What You Don't Know About Social Media *Can* Hurt You:

Take Control of Your Online Reputation

by
Kerry Rego

Thank you
for your support!

What You Don't Know About Social Media *Can* Hurt You:
Take Control of Your Online Reputation

ISBN-13: 978-0615705576

First printing: December 2012

Editor/Proofreader: Cheri Lieurance

Cover Designer: Chelsea McKenna Design

Trademarks
All terms mentioned in this book are known to be trademarks or service marks have been appropriately capitalized. Use of a term in this book should not be regarded as affecting the validity of any trademark or service mark.

Warning and Disclaimer
Every effort has been made to make this book as complete and as accurate as possible, but no warranty or fitness is implied. The information provided is on an "as is" basis. The author shall have neither liability nor responsibility to any person or entity with respect to any loss or damages arising from the information contained in this book.

Sales
You may order more copies of this book at the following address:
http://kerryregoconsulting.com/blog/books/ or by emailing
book@kerryregoconsulting.com.

Speaking
If you would like to invite the author to speak in support of this book's subject matter, please email speaker@kerryregoconsulting.com.

I dedicate this book to my loving husband, Dan.
You are my opposite. You are all the things I am not and more.
You are the one who makes all this possible.
I am grateful for your friendship, love, and support.

I also dedicate this book to my sassy little one, Joy.
For you I achieve. For you I set an example of strong womanhood.
One of my biggest goals in life is to make you proud of me.

ACKNOWLEDGEMENTS

Colleen Dillaway – I am grateful to have the love, guidance, friendship, and humor of our sisterhood. I'm lucky you are <u>mine</u>.

Short List/Sassy B's – The ladies who are there for me in every form of communication. I am grateful we found each other. My life is sassier with you in it.

Katie Berhorst – Thank you for your dedication to the English language, being a great friend, your willingness to read my book, and mark the manuscript with your sage pen.

John DeGaetano – Without your guidance in the creation of this book, it wouldn't exist.

Santa Rosa Small Business Development Center – Your small business program and services have helped me immeasurably.

Oxford comma – My friend, Katie, reintroduced us and gave me the confidence to use you again. I missed you.

ABOUT THE AUTHOR

Kerry Rego is a Social Media trainer, technology consultant, and keynote speaker that works with individuals, businesses, government, and non-profits. She educates, implements, and trains people of all ages on new media tools. Kerry is the County of Sonoma Social Media staff trainer, City of Santa Rosa Recreation and Parks Department Social Media instructor, lead trainer for the California Community College grant funded Interactive Internet Mobile Applications for Business program (IIMA4BIZ), a North Bay Business Journal contributing author, and a Vistage International speaker. She is a recipient of the North Bay Business Journal's 2011 "Forty Under 40 Award".

Kerry started her adventure with technology on a Commodore 64 and a Texas Instrument TI-99/4A. She has 30 years of personal computer experience, 18 years as a multiple subject matter trainer, 17 years of corporate use on both PC and Mac, and has been training in her current capacity for 6 years. Technology continually excites her and it never gets old.

Kerry is based out of Santa Rosa, CA in beautiful Sonoma County, an hour north of San Francisco. She was born there and makes it her home with her husband and daughter.

People and tech together, changing the world.

TABLE OF CONTENTS

Chapter 5: Resources
- Books
- Blogs
- Other resources
  - Sample editorial calendar
  - Sample metric report

Bibliography
Kerry Rego Consulting Services
Testimonials
I Want to Hear From You

INTRODUCTION

As a Social Media and technology trainer, my job is to educate on how to work with the tools available, how to express your message and character, and guide you in effective use of your time on the web. I have noticed my clients are growing more and more nervous about the information we find when working together. They are shocked that so much of their personal (and often incorrect) information is floating out there.

As time marches on, the evidence suggests to me that this subject is important enough to warrant a book and regular presentations that address legal issues and other obstacles, concerns, and changes in the industry. I also offer, within this book and during my seminars, action items to help take some control over what is readily available about you on the web. This book is for those who want takeaways or want to share what they have learned with others.

Eric Schmidt, the former CEO of Google, famously said at the Techonomy conference in Lake Tahoe on August 8, 2010, "Every 48 hours internet users create more content than all the content that ever existed from the dawn of civilization to 2003."[1] Let me allow you to wrap your brain around that statistic. He said this in 2010 and it only includes information up to 2003. The exponential growth in the meantime is downright overwhelming.

I want to teach you how to surf the tidal wave of all that data.

WHO CAN USE THIS BOOK

Everyone who would like to know more about protecting their online reputation can find value in this book. Additionally, I frequently encounter people who tell me they aren't interested in using Social Media or that it isn't appropriate for communicating with their clients. This book is designed with them in mind. With no disrespect, I call these people **"doubters."** The doubters often feel this way about Social Media. They:

- Don't like it
- Don't get it
- Don't believe in it
- Don't understand it
- Don't want to use it

I am passing no judgment. My goal is not to convert you to using it. (Please don't get upset that I'm pro-Social Media and new media. It's my job!) I am here to give you information you're probably not going to get otherwise. I am hoping this book was given to you by a colleague, employee, friend, or family member that was concerned you are being excluded or damaged by your lack of knowledge on the subject.

This book isn't designed to train you to use Facebook, LinkedIn, Twitter, or some other Social Media tool. I wrote it so that you know the limitations of the current methods you are using to communicate with your customers, prospective clients, and the public in general. Additionally, this book isn't designed to cover every subject mentioned in detail. Yes, there is more out there but this is intended to give you a good grasp on the landscape. Business has changed and I want you to have the information you need to stay in the game.

I wrote this book to:

- Give you practical information about current methods and help you understand some of their restrictions
- Make sure you understand what's at stake
- Help you understand the legal and privacy concerns of using new and Social Media

- Provide you with actionable steps that will allow you to invest the minimum amount of money and time required to manage your reputation online
- Give you the confidence to stand your ground when someone challenges you about why you aren't using a particular Social Media tool and the knowledge that your decision was based on sound evidence rather than fear of the unknown

AN IMPORTANT NOTE ABOUT
WHY I AM SHARING THIS INFORMATION

A lot of people want to know how I can write a book that reveals many of the tactics I use to help protect my clients' reputations and still keep my business doors open. If every person who read my book were to have the passion, time, and money to put into practice the techniques I lay out here, then I wouldn't have a job. The truth is, most do not. I am hired because I achieve the same results (or better) than they would, in less time.

I hope you are someone with the time and the willingness to take action on what I put into these pages. I hope that you read this and take it to heart. That's why I wrote it. I want to arm you with the knowledge I have so that you can make sure you and your business are safer online than when you opened this book. This information is not proprietary; there are some firms that won't share with you, but I want you to be able to protect your name.

CHAPTER 1:

YOUR REPUTATION
IS AT RISK

WHAT IS REPUTATION MANAGEMENT?

Wikipedia defines Reputation Management as "the practice of understanding or influencing an individual or business brand. It was originally coined as a public relations term, but advancement in computing, the internet, and Social Media made it primarily an issue of search results."[2]

When you ponder the subject of Reputation Management, I'd like you to consider the following questions:

- **What are people saying about you and your brand?**
- **What are the perceived opinions about you?**
- **What is your character?**
- **Are you trustworthy?**
- **Are you good at what you do?**
- **What is the general public going to find when they look up your name on the internet?**

Have you ever "Google'd" yourself?

This term is a brand-specific word for the action of looking up your name on the web, also called a vanity search. When people research you or your company on the internet, what are they going to find? This is a scary thought full of the unknown. But it doesn't have to be if you know how to exert some control over what is found. I'm not talking about spending thousands of dollars to sanitize your reputation or boost your website in search engines. Those services are available to you and you can certainly do that, if you like. The goal of this book is to provide you with extremely low-cost ways of making sure that the first few pages of any search engine results are filled with items you've written, created, or are under your control. When I say "low-cost," I mean it. The majority of tools and solutions listed here are FREE. That's right – free. It will only take a plan (**see Chapter 4: Strategy and Action Items**) and some time. We're not talking about hours and hours of your life. It will require some time to build the structure and a little bit of maintenance on a regular basis.

~

YOUR PERSONAL REPUTATION

It's not <u>if</u> someone researches you online, it's <u>when</u>.

Some years ago, I was talking to the police chief of a city in Sonoma County, and when he learned what I did for a living, he mentioned that during job interviews, he'd hand the keyboard to the interviewee and ask the person to navigate to his or her Social Media sites and show past behavior. This police department may no longer do this, but the story stuck with me. As a keynote speaker, I talk about this possibility to adults as well as teenagers and this is a point I drive home no matter who is in the audience.

Here are just some of the things that we look at on an online profile that help us make decisions about whether or not we want to hire you, admit you into college, go on a date with you, add you to our network, or use your services:

Headshot, not a sexy shot.

Your photo

The picture of you with an excessively large beer in your hand isn't helping anyone. Neither is the picture of your favorite celebrity. I'm also uncomfortable seeing so much of your cleavage. This goes for guns, nudity, skimpy clothing/bathing suits, really old photos that no longer look like you and kissy faces.

Your photo is more than just a way for you to express who you are and what you're about. It's the way you are perceived by the world. You can still be unique!

Action: A smiling headshot is the best solution. You can invest in a professional photographer but you don't need to. Anyone you know with a high quality camera (or a smartphone) can help you get this shot. Pay attention to your background, make sure the lighting is hitting your face rather than behind you, and be aware of your choice of wardrobe. Take shots until you have two or three that you like. Use the same shot in multiple places online because your face is your calling card and people will recognize you based on these images. Upload pictures that your boss/grandma/mom/mentor wouldn't cringe at seeing. Why? Because the odds are, one of them **will** see it.

My Impotrant Buzinss

Spelling

Your second grade teacher was right. Spelling matters. I've seen a woman who spelled *the name of her own company wrong.* If you can't write in a clear, correct, and concise manner, this will give me (and many others) pause about your abilities on a larger scale. Knowing this is your reputation, and the fact that you can't be bothered to spellcheck or have someone review for errors, tells us it simply isn't important to you and we infer much from that lackadaisical approach.

Action: Have a trusted person review your profiles for basic spelling, contextual appropriateness, and grammatical errors. This person doesn't need to use the red pencil approach. Just ask the reviewer to take five minutes to examine it and point out any errors. Pick someone who is known for good communication skills.

Style of communication

Have you ever read a profile for a person who was overly confident? This occurs frequently on LinkedIn, and when a person tries too hard to sound competent, it comes off as cocky. Consider this paraphrased description for a person you may want to hire or work with: "I am a marketing master that dominates all others in the field. You must hire me or your business will fail miserably." When this one backfires, it reflects so poorly on the writer, the person often can't recover respect on any level.

Action: This solution is the same as for spelling. Have someone you respect review your profile. Her notes on your style will do wonders for your presentation. Try to listen without becoming defensive.

Damaging information

The information available to us on the web is vast and sometimes negative. If you have enemies or particularly spiteful competitors, they can say anything they want about you on the internet. It's up to you to know that it's out there and that there are ways to combat incorrect information.

Several years ago, a realtor who I'll call Joe Taylor, came to me with a problem. A displeased customer had written a negative blog about Joe's services years before and Joe was understandably upset that this blog post was still showing up in the number one spot on Google. Before I met with him, I researched him and was unable to find his website. I asked Joe if he had one and he said he did not. In this example, Joe was simply putting up with negativity by sitting back and letting someone else drive his reputation. It didn't matter if the blog was true or not, if it's the only information someone finds to go on, this is what they will believe.

My recommendation for Joe was to buy a domain based on his name such as http://www.joetaylor.com and build even a basic website to start with to make sure that when someone looked up his name, his website would be among the top results. The simple act of having one's own website is very powerful in the eyes of search engines. In addition, I would have had him create his own blog and use a few other tools (**see Chapter 4: Strategy and Action Items**) to bump that inaccurate blog down the list.

The negative blog had two advantages. One, it was the only information available. Two, the writer chose to use Blogger which is owned by Google. The search engine does heavily promote it's own content. If you are using any social Google tools, they will make sure it's visible. Any proactive action on this man's part would've been beneficial. Needless to say, he was looking for a magic solution in the form of paying someone to make the negative blog go away and he didn't hire me. Sorry folks, it doesn't work that way anymore. You do have to put in a little effort.

Action: Create your own content to replace the negative information available. **See Chapter 4: Strategy and Action Items.**

*Bonus issue: If you have a personal email address that is "hottiewithbody@gmail.com" or "smokin420@yahoo.com" this is doing tremendous damage to your reputation. No one will take you seriously with this kind of communication channel. I normally have to address this with teenagers, but it doesn't hurt to tell you as well. In the next section, I address owning your own domain name, and I recommend that if you purchase your own domain, that you set up an email address based on it.
Examples for me: kr@kerryrego.com or kerry@kerryrego.com.

Duplicate names

I personally know of at least two people who share a name with a performer in the porn industry. One is an actress that, upon arriving at an audition, was told by a casting director that they almost didn't call her in after what they found during an internet search. The only reason she got the audition is because the adult performer was of a different race than her, and it was easy to tell from the pictures available online that they were different people. The average person will see something like that and run the other way.

When I looked up the name Susan Smith, how many results did I find? Oh, only 68,700,000. But there are ways to help those looking find the right Susan!

Action: Perform a vanity search on your name to see if there are others who share it. Make sure you own your name in the form of a domain, such as http://www.yourname.com. If that isn't possible, try variations of your name like adding your middle name or initial. You can try adding your industry, such as using http://www.yournameplusindustry.com. For Susan it might be http://www.SusanSmithSpeechPathology.com. You could even do it by location, such as http://www.SusanSmithSanDiego.com. You can own multiple domains and point them all to the same website, if you like, so buy as many as you can if your name is common.

When there are pictures uploaded of you on the staff page of your website, on your profile bio, or other locations, make sure the picture file is your name. When your name is searched on the internet, image files come up in those searches, and it will help those who don't know you differentiate you from others with your same name.

There are many places to purchase domains. These are just a few of them:

- http://www.godaddy.com
- http://www.domain.com
- http://www.namecheap.com

~

CONSEQUENCES FOR THE INDIVIDUAL

Let's explore some ways your online reputation can affect your personal life.

Job Market

In a 2010 study by Microsoft and Cross Tab Market Research, 70 percent of U.S. recruiters have rejected candidates based on their online reputation, while only 7 percent of Americans believe their online reputation affects their job search. According to Eurocom Worldwide, "Almost one in five technology industry executives say that a candidate's Social Media profile has caused them not to hire that person."

Almost 40% of the companies surveyed check potential employees' Social Media profiles.[3]

You may say, "I don't use Social Media, so I'm fine." But here's a fact that may scare you, Did you know if you own an Android phone* or tablet, you automatically get assigned a Google+ profile? It's true. Your Google+ profile shows up very high when you search on Google. It's their latest social product and they are heavily promoting it to compete with Facebook and Twitter. In the second quarter of 2012, Google's Android phones surged to 68 percent market share[4] (sales figures, not ownership). Even if you don't fit into this category, there are other profiles out there assigned to you and your name **that you didn't set up.**

*You may not be sure what type of smartphone you own. There are only a few types, and if you're not sure which you own, here is a rundown: Apple, of course, makes the iPhone. Google Android phones are made by several manufacturers such as HTC, Samsung, LG, and Motorola. Windows phones are made by Nokia, Dell, LG, and HTC. Even though Research in Motion's Blackberry phones were the first to be successful in this category, they now only have approximately 5 percent of the market and are effectively out of the game.

Do you remember me mentioning talking to a chief of police about reviewing online content during a job interview? What's important about this story is that you understand what they did is fairly common but not illegal. They did not ask for passwords, an act which *is* illegal under the Stored Communications Act (SCA) and/or the Computer Fraud and Abuse Act (CFAA)[5]. There was quite a bit of upset over the idea of employers requiring log-in credentials of their prospective hires. This really wasn't the case; it was a story that snowballed and took on a life of its own, but it is an important conversation for us to have. Many members of Congress wanted to pursue legislation banning this practice but as it is already in place, that's largely unnecessary.

The point here is that when applying for a job, a background check will occur. These checks are now including searches on the internet in addition to checking your references, credit, criminal history, driving history, and more. Which is the first check you think will be performed?

If you already have a job, Social Media can still affect you negatively. People have called in sick then been caught having a great time when they were supposed to be ill. **Fired**. Polarizing personal opinions have been mistakenly posted to corporate accounts. **Fired**. Sometimes people think it's a good idea to send inappropriate photos to others and (oopsy Congressman Anthony Weiner!) send them using a public method. **Fired**.

Credit checks

Financial institutions need to understand the risk profiles of their borrowers. They will take advantage of all information available to them in the pursuit of this data. Credit scores are approximately 60 days behind current activity. Banks are evaluating the risks of future defaults such as how you discuss new purchases, vacations, and spending behaviors. What's more current than Social Media data? Industry reports say the use of Social Media to fill out risk profiles is three to five years away[6] but that there are some institutions, such as Lenddo in the Philippines, that are already adopting these practices.

Legal

Law enforcement is using Social Media to monitor the communities they work in. Please don't break the law and, if you do, don't post about it on the web and be surprised when it comes back to bite you! I've heard some unbelievable stories including: a woman complained about the mold in her apartment and was sued by her landlord; one woman claimed disability, was photographed dancing on tables, and then sued by her insurance company; a young woman drove under the influence of alcohol, hit another vehicle, laughed about it on Facebook, and then went to jail for her refusal to remove the content from her account.

A woman that works for a county health department shared with me that her department regularly monitors Facebook for fraud. Recipients of government benefits, such as food stamps, have been known to offer them for sale to their social networking friends. You are not in a private setting and the things you write may be used against you in court. Use common sense about what you share.

Dating

Thank goodness I got married before search engines and social networks were something to worry about. Though I'm off the market, even I have used the web to investigate a mate on a friend's behalf. My friend and I attended a concert where I introduced her to the man she eventually married. While she was driving us home, she asked me took look up if he had a girlfriend. Due to the fact that he is well known, this was a valid request and I immediately checked his Wikipedia page. "No relationship listed." I said. I Google'd him for more info. I put in some hardcore effort on my friend's behalf for about 10 minutes, but no pictures of him with a significant other or information alluding to that fact were found.

With Facebook, Google, Instagram and other tools, people now have the opportunity to investigate a tremendous amount about you long before you actually say hello face-to-face.

Many people create multiple profiles on networks such as Facebook and LinkedIn in an attempt to separate personal and professional information or to elude detection by certain parties.

A warning: Creating multiple accounts on Facebook or LinkedIn is a violation of the stated terms of use and discovery of this could get you banned. I know that there are many people that do just this and some go undetected for years. If you have done so, the option of merging duplicate accounts is practically unheard of because having more than one is against the rules. These companies and services don't owe you anything. They won't warn you. They will simply shut you out and your email address will be banned from their system. You can create a new account with a brand new email address but all that data, connections, and history are gone forever.

There are settings that allow you to determine what your friends see on Facebook and I've tested the effectiveness to only find failure. I had four friend lists. I segregated a post to each list and asked in each that if "you can see this, like this post." For each test, I received likes from people on all of my lists. I did it from mobile as well as desktop. Needless to say, I don't trust the friend list privacy segregation settings. I say, if you can't say it to everyone, you should probably use another delivery mode outside of Facebook.

~

WHAT A COMPROMISED REPUTATION MEANS FOR YOUR BUSINESS

There are a variety of reasons that your business brand's reputation matters, including customer perception, market value, and your ability to attract top talent.

People have always told others when they received great or horrible service. We are social, community-based creatures and we recommend or dissuade our friends and family all day long. Social Media and the internet have given us more ways to publicly reward and shame businesses.

Imagine the very worst thing a person could say about your business:

- You provide terrible service
- You are overpriced
- They would never return and encourage others not to use your services
- Your product is defective

Not only does this affect your reputation, it can damage your stock value as well. According to Standard & Poor's 500 Index, your business reputation accounts for 31 percent of your stock value on average.[7] Consider the case study below.

Many years ago, I worked as a temporary employee while I auditioned for jobs as a model and actress. I worked for several staffing firms during that time and interviewed regularly for temp jobs as well as work in entertainment. When you work as a temporary employee and are a good hire, you get offered a lot of work. It was the first time in my life that I realized employees are interviewing the boss and the company as much as the other way around. Even when the economy is tough, hiring managers need to remember that jobs are a two way street. Employees may take a job that fits them right now but they are concerned about environment, morale, culture, growth and a good fit for them. They will leave if not treated right or if they receive a better opportunity.

One thing that must be clear: it can take decades to build the reputation of a business and a few comments from a "squeaky wheel" can bring it all crashing down. **See Chapter 3: Obstacles, Concerns, and Solutions** to learn ways to deal with negative customer feedback.

~

CASE STUDY

Dave Carroll and his band, Sons of Maxwell, were travelling by United Airlines on March 31, 2008 when another passenger noticed mishandling of baggage while looking through the window. Carroll's $3,500 Taylor guitar was damaged in the process. Though it only cost $1,200 to repair, the sound of the instrument was never the same.

After Carroll spent a full year attempting to receive compensation from United Airlines through traditional methods of customer service, he became fed up and decided to try a different route. As a musician, he had ample ability to be creative and chose to shoot three videos detailing the situation in a humorous way and then posted them to YouTube. Within one day, the video had over 150,000 views. As of the summer of 2012, the first video "United Breaks Guitars" had reached over 12 million views while the set of three had received more than 14 million views.

The airline issued a belated apology and $3,000 in compensation. Carroll requested it be donated to charity instead. United's stock price dropped 10 percent within four days of the video posting, costing stockholders $180 million, according to "The Times" (UK newspaper)[8]. There are many discussions on how much stock was truly lost and if it was a direct reflection of this public relations disaster.

CHAPTER 2:

THE NEW BUSINESS ENVIRONMENT

WHAT IS SOCIAL MEDIA?

Let's back up a minute. To be effective in managing your reputation online, you will need to have a basic understanding of the tools available and what they are about.

Social Media are online publishing tools that turn broadcast monologues into dialogues. The rules: it must be on the internet, allow conversation, and be shareable.

So often I hear people refer to Social Media as "social networking" when it so much more than that. I want you to see the variety of categories included in new media and that they aren't limited to tools that allow you to chat with your friends:

- Bookmarking
- News
- Networking
- Multimedia sharing sites (photo, video, and audio)
- Email marketing
- Blogs, microblogs, RSS feeds
- Content sharing, (customer review, Q&As, and docs)
- Location-based services
- Event marketing

There are even more tools that allow you to manage your Social Media marketing, advertising, intelligence, scoring, TV, games, shopping, and analytics. I won't go into these because they don't follow the tighter definition of Social Media and don't serve our purpose of understanding basic functions of the genre.

I want to explain what these functions are, how they can be used, and some websites that fit into these categories. **Please remember that there are not only many definitions for Social Media, some of these tools fit into multiple categories.** Some people would argue with me as to where they should be placed, and some of these tools may be purchased or phased out by the time you read this. Such is the nature of the web. Also, there are many more tools than the ones I've listed. I simply offer a list of the most popular services or names you may recognize. There are many more services that can be included in each list.

Bookmarking

Social bookmarking is the act of tagging a website and saving it for later. Whether you are sending it in an email or saving it on a website as part of a collection, you have bookmarked. The difference between bookmarking a website on your computer and social bookmarking is that with the latter, you are saving the item to the web and it can be shared with someone else.

How is this useful? Consider offering resources of information for clients, ideas for school projects, inspirations for branching out in new product directions, or visual presentations to name a few.

Sites: Digg, StumbleUpon, Reddit, Pinterest, Delicious

News

Social news websites feature stories that are posted by users and allow them to be ranked by others based on popularity. Posts can be commented upon and, in some cases, the comments are also open to ranking. Crowdsourcing allows this to show the collective intelligence of the users and allows for democratic information flow.

How is this useful? Rather than relying on traditional publishers to provide you with the most important news, you can source the crowd of internet users for what they think is important in a variety of categories including sports, humor, global affairs, economics, business and more.

Sites: Twitter, Slashdot, Fark, Delicious, Reddit, Newsvine

Networking

Social networking gets the most attention out of the group. It's the loudest, if you will. These websites and applications allow people to communicate with others or find those with similar interests. This serves to fulfill a basic social need. We must communicate with each other; it's the way we are wired.

How is this useful? When I ask people over the age of 50 how they talk to their kids, their answer is almost always Facebook. Really, I'm not kidding. Whether you are talking to a close family member, or someone on a far away branch of your family tree, these tools are powerful "connectors." Social networks are regularly bringing distant families together, reuniting childhood friends, and reigniting romantic relationships long thought to be expired.

I would be remiss if I didn't mention that this is increasingly a preferred form of communication for younger generations. Many of them don't answer the phone and don't use email. If you want to capture a younger market, you need to be where they are and they are frequently on social networks.

Sites: Facebook, LinkedIn, Orkut, Google+, Renren, Myspace

Multimedia sharing with photo, video, and audio

Social sharing occurs in many categories of Social Media, but the ability to share your digital pictures, video, and audio with others through websites and applications is one of the most popular functions on the web. The internet used to be text based, plain white (with practically no graphics), and it was quite tough on the eyes. Today's internet is in rich color, is visually appealing, and has excellent audio.

Digital photography and the availability of inexpensive cameras has dramatically increased the amount of photos we want to take, store, and share with others. Social tools help with the last two needs by offering massive amounts of free storage and a wide variety of ways to deliver our images to friends and family.

Videos require a tremendous amount of web space. Video-sharing sites or video-hosting sites are useful to everyone who owns their own website so that they don't have to store these dense files on their own servers at a significant cost. It also makes the process of multimedia uploading, editing, sharing or embedding very easy for the average person.

Audio has added another layer to our ability to share information in layers. The cost of equipment has drastically dropped while it's availability in the majority of handheld devices has increased. With minor investments in quality microphones, everyone can be a radio host (now called podcasters).

How is this useful? You can share photos from: your vacation, wedding, business expo, community service project, new baby photo shoot, amazing recipes, a project portfolio, staff images, beautiful locations, real estate listings and more. Potential video subjects include: a greeting from a business owner, product demonstration, first dance at your daughter's wedding, the first steps of a grandchild, the hole-in-one you caught with your phone camera, and anything else you can imagine. Audio is beneficial for interviews, answering audience questions, or if you are a better verbal communicator, you will be drawn to this solution.

Sites:
Photos – Flickr, Picasa, SmugMug, Instagram
Video – YouTube, Vimeo
Audio – Audioboo, iTunes, SoundCloud

Email marketing

In contrast to traditional paper mail, email marketing takes on a variety of visual and goal-oriented forms, but the main idea is that these services allow you to send email to a large quantity of people and be legally compliant.

It's important for you to know about the CAN-SPAM Act of 2003[9] (Controlling the Assault of Non-Solicited Pornography and Marketing Act), the first national standard for sending commercial email and it was signed into law by President George H.W. Bush. The Federal Trade Commission enforces this public law which allows marketers to send unsolicited email as long as it has: an unsubscribe feature, content, and sending behavior compliance. Sending to existing customers or anyone who has inquired about products or services, even if they haven't given specific permission, are exempt from the restrictions. The authorized financial penalty **per violation is $16,000.00.** The highest judgment ever obtained for violations was $900,000 against Jumpstart Technologies in 2006.

Spammers ignore this law and I know you get a tremendous amount of email that violates the rules. Just because others do it, would you be willing to put your business or reputation on the line to save a few dollars a month?

How is this useful? The benefits of using email marketing tools can include: ecommerce, multimedia, links, brilliant graphics, no need to open attachments, document sharing, analytic tracking, social sharing, events, surveys, and more.

The variety of services that are available to send email marketing messages are in compliance with the CAN-SPAM Act. If you send emails to large groups of people from your company domain email address, use a web-based email service such as Gmail or Yahoo!, or use a desktop email program like Outlook, you are not in compliance. You can send to a large number of people and you are charged based on the size of your email list. These services won't sell lists of email addresses to you: they are simply the postmen for messages you want to send to a list you already possess.

Let's say you wanted to send a marketing message to 1,000 people from your email address the same way you'd send to five people, there are some issues with that approach. Your internet service provider (ISP) has provided you with an account that allows a certain number of emails to pass through their pipes. The limits are different for each ISP, but after ten or twenty or one hundred, depending on their allowances, your ISP will put you on a watch list. If you regularly violate the number they've allotted for your service, you won't be able to send anymore. You have officially become a spammer. The same thing happens on the other end of the line. When the email goes out, the receiving ISP knows how many people were included on your email and they will demote your delivery reputation and you will be flagged in their system as well. Many of your emails will never be delivered to the intended recipients because you will be diverted into junk mail or spam folders.

By using an email marketing service, you can send to as many people as you like (permission-based please!) without losing your reputation or getting fined – what else do these tools offer you?

- Your flyer will be embedded, not an attachment
- Rich color
- Professionally designed templates
- Clickable links to websites
- Multimedia options
- Social Media share buttons allowing recipients to share your email with friends

- Tracking who opened the email (or didn't), who clicked on what link and when (you can then follow-up with a sales call)
- Tracking unsubscribes from your mailing list and the services will pull the addresses out for you
- Detailed reports on performance

Email marketing services are pretty amazing. Did I mention that sales conversion happens in email?

Sites: Constant Contact, Vertical Response, MailChimp, AWeber

Blog, microblogs, RSS feeds

A blog (shortened version of weblog) is an information site that allows you to post your thoughts and ideas. These posts are presented in reverse chronological order.

A microblog differs from a traditional blog in that it's shorter in length.

RSS feeds (RDF Site Summary or sometimes called Really Simple Syndication) allow you to subscribe to multiple blogs and view them in a standardized format in one location.

How is this useful? Having a blog is freedom of speech at its best. You, as either an individual or company, can express the mission of your organization, what's important to you, and what sets you apart from your competition. Additionally, it offers the ability for your voice to be heard whereas a static website is just that, static.

Search engines need to provide their audiences with a source of up-to-date information and blogs are the best way to do so. With the push of a button, you can send a press release to the whole world. Blogs drive traffic to your website and are the pages that search engines scan for a match when your prospective client enters the words that describe a business. If you own a carpet cleaning company, your blog (not to mention website) should have words like "carpet," "clean," "pad," "stain," "solution," and other words that your customer is going to use to search on the internet for a service provider. Those keywords bring people to your website.

Microblogs are more conversational and "right now." I call them link herders because I can herd readers to one site or another by providing them with a link. A blog is long form, as long as you want it to be. Microblogs have space limitations. This constraint forces you to become a better writer because you must capture the audience's attention quickly. Think newspaper headlines. This form of communication is easily accessible by any phone with the capacity to text and was used continuously in the revolutions seen around the globe in 2011-2012.

RSS feeds can save a tremendous amount of time when consuming information. If you are researching a particular subject and have found 25 excellent blogs, an RSS feed is like a television where you direct all the content to go so all you have to do is "turn on the TV" and all the channels you want to "watch" are there. Rather than navigating to each individual website/blog to see if it's been updated, you can find it all in one location. While RSS feeds were the preferred way for power users to access their favorite blogs in the past, they aren't used as much today because this function has been duplicated on other sites such as Facebook or LinkedIn where a newsfeed is common.

Sites:
Blogs – Wordpress, Blogger, Typepad, Tumblr
Microblogs – Twitter, Weibo
RSS feeds – Google Reader, Feedreader

Content sharing (customer review, Q&As, documents)

Content sharing is a general category of sites that allow you to share your opinion on a service, ask questions, or share media such as documents.

How is this useful? Customers are always going to share their opinions about services and businesses. Business owners now have the opportunity to overhear those conversations on review sites and even control (to some extent) the environment in which they are shared.

Question and answer sites are a great way for people to learn about a wide variety of concepts that they may find confusing or want to learn more about. As a representative of a business, you have the opportunity to answer questions about your product or service in addition to clarifying confusion.

Document sharing is particularly useful for teams. If you've ever worked on a document that has been passed from hand to hand, or emailed from person to person, the ability to edit a document online and keep it in one spot may appeal to you. It also helps prevent "version confusion." Many documents can be difficult to email due to their size and document sharing can eliminate that aggravation. Visual artists, authors, and musicians who create intellectual property have the opportunity to host their creations online and send a link to someone who wants to view it. Examples of documents include but aren't limited to: portfolios, music files, pictures, videos, screencasts, PDFs, ebooks, whitepapers, reports, slideshows, drawings, and educational materials.

Sites:
Customer review – Yelp, Merchant Circle, Trip Advisor
Q&A – Quora, Yahoo! Answers
Document share – Google Docs/Drive, Behance, Scribd, Slideshare

Location-based services

This is a general program-level service that uses the global positioning system chip in mobile devices to provide information or entertainment based on the user's position on the planet.

How is this useful? Sometimes this function is represented in a game and sometimes it's presented as an answer to a search for information.

Gamification[10] is the use of game mechanics and design techniques in non-game contexts. It's a psychological manipulation to get people to do things. This can also be referred to as a "call to action". What makes gamification more effective at behavior modification than a simple call to action is that it may offer a reward. The reward can come in the form of more playing time, a virtual item such as a badge, points or bragging rights with the use of a leader board. People will jump through hoops for real (or virtual) gold stars.

Many of these services have a check-in feature for checking in at specific locations for benefits. There's a valid concern about telegraphing your location and being vulnerable as a result. Choosing very carefully where and when you share that information with the world is a common sense approach. If you test one of these services, don't share that you will be out of town for two weeks or you may come home to a very empty house or business!

Business owners can create an account that awards a coupon to customers on their first visit (or for repeats), for performing specific tasks, or for providing up-to-date information on specials or products. Location-based services are important to be aware of because your customers are frequently looking for your physical address or contact information online, often while mobile. Your business may have been mapped incorrectly. The importance of accuracy is the difference between a happy customer and one who is upset because the information provided to them was wrong. Google+ Local is used by other websites and applications to give directions and maps to consumers. If that one's wrong, you could be in trouble.

Sites: Google+ Local, foursquare, Facebook check in feature, Path

*Excerpt from "Gamification: The Greatest Call to Action" published on my blog and available here: http://kerryregoconsulting.com/2012/11/07/gamification-the-greatest-call-to-action/

Event marketing

These are tools that are designed to help you invite people to an event (whether physical or virtual), allow guests to share the event with others, and even implement ecommerce.

How is this useful? If you've ever hosted an event, you know they can be a challenge. With event marketing tools, you can create a digital invitation with color, graphics, multimedia, maps and more that can be shared via email or Social Media. They can include the following functions: RSVP, payments, ticketing, receipts, reminder messages, tagging people, check-in, guest lists, follow-up communications, feedback collection, analytics, and the ability to repeat the process again and again.

Sites: Eventbrite, Constant Contact, Evite, Facebook Events

~

THE BENEFITS OF USING SOCIAL MEDIA

I'm called to the mat regularly to answer this question. My answer to "Why should I use Social Media?" is a little round-about.

Social media is not magic.
It will not fix a broken product.

You must have a goal and vision for your organization. You must know your target audience. You must provide a great product and excellent customer service. Business hasn't changed so much that these basic tenets have gone away. New and Social Media only aid your endeavors.

That said, there is a long list of reasons why Social Media can be of benefit to you and your company. Since we're here and discussing it, I'll give you those reasons. You may stick with your original feelings about the subject, and I may not change your mind. I do want you to have the information so that you can make an informed decision based on facts and reason rather than fear. (Sorry, I had to say it.) We'll get into fear in **Chapter 3: Obstacles, Concerns, and Solutions**.

Before I answer, I'll pose a question of my own:

Are you planning on retiring in the next three years?

- If "**Yes,**" then don't worry. You won't need Social Media or any other massive online investment due to the time it would take to recoup.
- If "**No,**" then I say "You should prepare for retirement or expect a significant loss of business over the next five years." If you choose not to keep pace with your clients, they will walk away from you.

The simple answer is, **it's the cost of doing business today.**[11] Your customers are using it and if you don't, you **will** suffer the consequences. There are many in industries such as law, finance, mortgage lending, and healthcare and these are what I call "classic" fields. They have done business a certain way for a very long time. It's working for them, so why change it? They don't have to. No one **has** to use Social Media (unless you are a restaurant, retailer, gaming company or the like. Do you get where I'm going with this?).

I heard an explanation that was so groundbreaking (to me) in its eloquence; I simply have to share it with you. In fact, I've been using it ever since I first heard it.

In the winter of 2011, I was sitting on a soundstage in a TV studio on the Los Angeles Valley College campus next to Steve Wright. I am the lead trainer for a California Community Colleges initiative called Interactive Internet and Mobile Applications for Business (http://www.web4biz.org) and Steve is the grant coordinator. We had been recording web videos of curriculum for several days and during a section of one-on-one conversation between the two of us, he said something that almost made me fall out of my chair.

"You know 40 years ago, when you started a business, you got a location and a phone line and you were in business. **No one ever asked the ROI of a phone.**" he said. I was stunned with the simplicity and accuracy of this observation. Steve worked in the phone industry for almost 24 years and I highly respect his insights on traditional business. It made me look at the telephone, and the rest of our communication tools, much differently.

So what are those reasons again?

Brand exposure and visibility

Unless you have a public relations firm and a large advertising budget for traditional methods of marketing and advertising, you may not be able to obtain the exposure and visibility that new and Social Media can afford you. It is largely free (though you can choose to spend a lot of money on it) and only requires manpower to post and maintain. In my opinion, the amount of time it takes is greatly overestimated.

As an individual, you are your brand. Market yourself much the same way a company would market a product. If you are looking for work, your employers are researching you online and the information available to them is what they are going to believe.

Highlight your product

These tools allow you to describe your product or services through multimedia and other interactive ways, at a length that isn't possible via traditional means. It also gives you the opportunity to clarify what your services are if there are any misconceptions.

Your skill set as an individual must be clearly defined. What value do you bring to the table? It's not easy to toot your own horn, I know. We aren't taught to communicate about ourselves that way. But I'm telling you, if you don't, who will? If what you do and how you do it is in your head, make sure it's clear on the page.

Tell your story and humanize the brand

People want to do business with people – with their neighbors and people they like – not brands or logos. You have the opportunity to tell the story of the employee who's been with your company for 40 years and the wonderful service he provides to your clients. This isn't something that will make it into the phone book, press release, or your brochure. Social Media and the extensive communication it can achieve allow your customers to identify with the people who work there rather than the building they see as they drive by.

I know plenty of people just like you. How can I tell the difference between you and the next person with your same credentials? You have to paint a picture for me. Show me your personality, your quirky nature. There can be a sense of reticence about being too personal or showing who you really are but try to go out of your comfort zone a bit. Confirm you are on the right path by showing your true colors to a trusted source before releasing to the wide world.

Build your sphere of influence

When you are able to clearly communicate what is important to you or your company, your customer and the public grow to know you intimately. Your words travel far and wide. It takes time for you to see the results but if you regularly put in the effort, you **will** see the aftereffects. You are an expert at what you do, so share what you know, and the public will understand the level of your expertise and recommend you to others as an authority in your field.

Communicate with other influencers and thought leaders

We never stop growing. The increased ability to communicate with others in our field is a wonderful benefit. Right now you may be attending annual conferences or educational seminars. But those only happen periodically. You now have the capacity to talk to anyone in your field, comparable industries, an area you want to expand into, or those you simply respect anytime you want. If you are passionate about what you do, you will have more opportunities to "geek out" about what you love with others who understand exactly what you are talking about. You can find a mentor and gain support of colleagues. When you spend time doing this, you will be inspired to think in new ways and be challenged to grow.

Network faster

Our networks are simply people we know. A hundred years ago if I needed a fence built, I'd think about whom I knew that had the skills to get the job done and ask for help. If I didn't know anyone who could do it personally, I'd ask for opinions or for a suggestion. Things haven't changed so much. With the added benefit of stored database information, I know more people, can search for the person with either the skill set I need or those that have the ability to connect me to the right person, and I can do it at a speed never before matched.

I hear lots of people say that Facebook isn't good for networking. Facebook is most commonly used by families and friends who want to stay connected to each other, have fun online, and to share entertaining content. The people using Facebook aren't in the business mindset. The reason many businesses use it is because that's where their customers are spending time. LinkedIn is your golden ticket when it comes to professional networking. LinkedIn is generally misunderstood and underused. I could literally talk for hours about its value in business to business (B2B) networking, communications, and intelligence gathering. I wanted to clarify that there are differences between the tools in all aspects because when networking is your goal, you must choose your channel wisely. They are not all created equal.

Get found on the web

The main purpose of a search engine (Google, Yahoo!, Bing, Blekko, AOL, etc.) is to provide the freshest search results possible. If you want to be found "on the first page of Google" as most people put it, you will need to use some forms of Social Media. In April 2012, Google put into place the Penguin update. This was a reconfiguration of the algorithms that are designed to weed out low-quality results from a natural search engine results page (SERPs). Google wants to get rid of web spam and Social Media use helps Google more quickly spot the junk. Thus, your Social Media tools are highly seen (and served to the public as search results) because they are trusted sources of new information.

Individuals, please remember that background checks for new hires are standard but they are now including Social Media channel reviews as well.

Transparency

This sounds like a buzzword, I know. But it's increasingly important for business people and organizations to be open and honest about their actions. New media marketing author Brian Solis says, "In a transparent, globalized economy, there is increasingly no such thing as private behavior. Nearly everything that happens inside companies can be forwarded, tweeted, or blogged about."[12] It **will** be talked about so make sure you say it first to get the jump on it. This is especially true if it could be construed incorrectly, public opinion is out of step with the reality of the situation, or it's truly negative. This allows you to go on the offense rather than defense. Strategically, offense is a better position. Additionally, with today's myriad of communication options, if you choose not to communicate about something, automatically you look like you're hiding something.

Your customers are using it

It doesn't matter if it's retail, telephone services, hospitality, cable, banking, food and beverage, utilities, or healthcare, your clients and customers are using Social Media to **talk to you and about you**. If you aren't talking back to them, you are effectively ignoring their pleas and requests for service. According to Pew Internet[13], 66 percent of online adults use social networking sites.

Two thirds of your adult audience is actively engaged in social internet activities whether or not you are using it.

Sixty percent of consumers are looking to the internet to check prices at competing stores, get directions to physical locations, and to read reviews of products, according to a study by Google and Compete.[14] Let's call this one simply: **lead conversion**.

Customer service

Ninety-three percent of Americans surveyed in the 2012 American Express® Global Customer Service Barometer say that companies fail to exceed their service expectations.[15] I say, any opportunity a company has to provide better service is an opportunity worth exploring.

There are piles of statistics I could share with you to support the concept of using Social Media to provide great service but I think these are the most useful (also from the American Express® Global Customer Service Barometer):

Consumers who have used social media for customer service do it for a number of reasons. The "Social Top 5" activities for these Americans are:

1. Seeking a response from a company about a service issue 50%
2. Praising a company for a great service experience 48%
3. Sharing information about your service experience with a wider audience 47%
4. Venting frustration about a poor service experience 46%
5. Asking other users how to have better service experiences 43%

In other words, your customers are seeking a great experience. They will be talking about it good or bad. Make sure you are a part of the conversation.

Sense of Community

Corporate Social Media use can provide a sense of community for your customers so that they can discuss and enjoy your products and services together. You may also take the opportunity to engage in a little research and development while you ask questions or survey your customers.

Develop company culture

You aren't just looking for new customers or a healthier bottom line. You are also looking to attract top talent. When I got out of college, I was a temporary employee for several staffing firms and learned something valuable about looking for work. Employers aren't the only ones making the choice. Employees are making their decisions based on factors such as company culture, working styles, environment, team communication, and more when they are choosing to work for a company. No matter the economic climate, a company has to be attractive to secure great employees.

Your potential hires are investigating your reputation in a variety of ways and you can bet they've done much of their research online.

Your competition is using it

Have you investigated your competitors lately? Do you know much about their product line, marketing, talent, or pricing? You should. It allows you to differentiate yourself, your service or product from the pack. If you are listening to the signals on Social Media, you will know when they are about to deploy a new product, are going under, or are about to shift focus. Pay attention.

Just a few industries that have been completely upended by new and Social Media include: publishing, news, entertainment, law enforcement, public relations, marketing, customer service, and human resources.

~

HOW TO MEASURE RETURN ON INVESTMENT

Social Media use is far more measurable than marketing methods in the past. The amount of analytics we can now review and research is endless. I have a few basic ROI calculations that you can start with for now.

The first is: You already track every dollar that lands on your ledger, right? Add one column or field that tracks how customers walked into your door or what influenced their purchasing decision. Simple.

Here's another way:

<u>Gross Profit – Marketing Investment</u>
Marketing Investment

Swap out Gross Profit and replace with Customer Lifetime Value, if you like. This is the measure of the profit generated by a single customer (or set thereof) during the course of the customer's relationship with your company.

Customer Lifetime Value – Marketing Investment
Marketing Investment

Remember when I talked about "no one ever measured the ROI of a phone"? It's true. No one ever thought to question the importance of having the most basic communication device readily available in your place of business.

Let's try an exercise.

What is your favorite way(s) to communicate?

- The telephone
- Letter writing
- Face to face
- Texting
- Emailing
- Instant messaging
- Facebook
- Twitter
- Google+
- Fax
- Morse code

All right. You got me. The last one was a joke. My point is that each person reading this book is going to pick a different method of communication or a combination of several. Your answer will vary depending on the purpose, of course. My choice largely depends on context, audience, and importance or immediacy of the message

What's my preference? The best way to reach me is by text. I prefer face-to-face when I want to get things done or am trying to learn more about someone (personally or professionally). I rely heavily on non-verbal cues to know what someone is really thinking. I prefer email for client communications because I can print it and refer to it later.

Remember this:

- Everyone is different
- The tool you choose depends on your end goal
- The telephone isn't the only game in town

Bonus point: Texting has a 98 percent open rate[16]. It's hands down the most effective delivery method of communicating today. And it's **not** just for young people.

I have included a metric report (**see Chapter 5: Resources**) created in Excel that I give to my clients to help them track the performance of their individual channels (I use it myself). It does take some time to manually enter the information; the fewer channels you use, the faster it is. The purpose is to see over time how your efforts are benefitting you. You will be surprised by the results (there's always something unexpected) and it will show you a Social Media platform that simply isn't paying off.

~

BUT YOU DON'T NEED SOCIAL MEDIA; YOU'RE IN THE PHONE BOOK

When you meet someone and are curious to learn more about that person or are thinking about using the services of a business, which of these are you more likely to do?

- Look them up in the phone book
- Ask your friends and colleagues what they think
- Look them up online to see what you can find

Peer opinion is extremely important in purchasing decisions but let's compare the first and last options for obtaining factual information. Eighteen states have enacted an opt-in policy for delivery of a phone book and only 2 percent of customers in those states choose to receive their copy.[17] Only people who are paid subscribers to landline phone services receive full-size phone books. Most people aren't aware that this is true. The thin directories we get are from secondary companies and don't include as much information as the ones directly from phone companies. We know we've been receiving phone books for our whole lives but never thought about how they got to our front steps prior to delivery.

The usage of landline phones is declining. In fact, the Technical Advisory Committee (TAC) advised the Federal Communications Commission (FCC) in July 2011 to pick a date to sunset the public switched telephone network (we call them landlines).[18] This is a huge decision with many facets and is far from decided, but the fact that they are having the conversation at all is important for you to know. As of 2012, up to 17 states, as well as AT&T and Verizon[19], are pushing for the end to a universal service obligation known as "provider of last resort." This would mean the removal of requirements for phone companies to provide service to everyone in a defined service area. This is a scary notion for the elderly and those living in rural areas where wireless service is unreliable. Natural disasters and other events that will affect our communication channels will be a major issue without a centralized system.

As traditional phone services disappear, the printed phone book will be considered a relic of the past. But since there's time before that happens, let's look at the service they provide.

Phone directories offer a vast resource of information about our communities that doesn't require electricity or an internet connection, are usable by people of all ages, and require no technical know-how other than literacy.

So what's the downside to using or advertising in the phone book? The information is only collected once per year. If you change your phone number or some other vital piece of information, you have to wait as long as one full year before it's updated. Thousands of people are relying on that information that is now incorrect. Let's say you miss the deadline or your account rep doesn't get your new info to the editor. Your friends or customers are not going to know your new phone number or physical address for **two years**! What happens if there is a typo?

Then there is cost. Prices vary widely based on your service, location, and size of the listing or ad. You could put a beautiful full-size ad (or a variety of other sizes) in a book, but it could cost you as much as a house. My friend Kevin owned a very successful business that restored homes after disasters. He told me that his phone directory bill was $1 million per year. He also added that he netted $12 million per year from that investment. At the time, he deemed it worth the cost. But with declining usage, he says that's no longer the case.

Small businesses that use only a cell phone or VOIP (voice over internet protocol) phone number like Skype or Google Voice, don't have the option of being listed in a traditional phone book. Companies that distribute yellow page directories are losing listings, as well as customers and advertisers, as people are more frequently choosing mobile-only options. A 2011 National Health Interview Survey (NHIS) indicated 31.6 percent of American homes had only wireless telephones during the first half of 2011—an increase of 1.9 percentage points since the second half of 2010[20].

What are the online options?

Listing your name or business name online is quick. With most sites, you can have a complete listing within 10 minutes. Many of them will use a confirmation process that involves mailing you a postcard with PIN number requiring you to use it when logging in. This is to make sure that the address you've listed is in fact where you are. It prevents a person from fraudulently listing a name or business name in a far-flung or incorrect location, on a massive scale. Imagine your worst enemy registering your name in Timbuktu on hundreds of internet directories in one day. Many of the well-known services require a confirmation process to slow down those with malicious intent.

Online directories are regularly free. You can pay for enhanced services but it's definitely not necessary. You can have your name and business name in dozens of "phone books" for free. Now remember, traditional phone books are location-based. Tampa information isn't given to citizens of Baton Rouge. With web-based directories, anyone in the world, regardless of location, can access your information. By maximizing the use of internet-based services, you increase your global reach at an exponential rate.

Many of the internet services such as Google+ Local (previously known as Google Places and Google Maps) and Yelp have multimedia options. You can include address, phone number, websites, services, pictures, video, links to other websites, keywords that lead people to you, and "your story." No traditional phone book in the world can do that.

Getting yourself listed in web directories has another benefit that printed phone books can't touch. The information contained in listings on major services such as Google+ Local are used on other websites as plug-ins or added maps and by decision engines that scrape data to provide you with results. So when you look up a local Chinese food restaurant, the odds are, the info is coming from an online directory rather than the restaurant's website. **See Chapter 4: Strategy and Action Items.**

~

WAYS THAT SOCIAL MEDIA WILL AFFECT YOU WHETHER YOU USE IT OR NOT

We've already talked about how the decline in landline users has reduced the number of people using the traditional phone book. They won't be able to look up your information in a book because they won't get one. Their only option will be to look you up on the web. If you haven't provided your information online, the odds are, someone else already has.

Have you heard of Google Street View[21]? Since 2007, Google has made a point of recording panoramic views and information about businesses and locations all over the globe. Your business or home has been recorded and is available to anyone who types the address into Google's search engine. **So your location already has a listing available to thousands of international viewers and potential clients (or stalkers) and it may or may not be correct.** And, yes, Google has been taken to court by parties and governments that believe this is an invasion of their personal or citizens' privacy. Whether or not the plaintiffs win, the damage has been done, and your information is out there.

If you book a room at the Las Vegas Palms Hotel, they may ask you for your Klout score. What is that? It's a measurement of your online influence. I don't believe that the service is accurate, but it's a measurement that many retailers are now referring to before deciding what level of service you receive.[22]

How does this really work? You check in at the Palms for vacation and are asked for your Twitter handle or some other verification platform. While you are admiring the chandelier, they are retrieving your Klout score. This is a number between 1 and 100 that will help them determine if you get a complimentary bottle of champagne, a VIP table at their nightclub, or a luxury suite. Your Klout number helps them understand how big your online audience is and how influential you are in the online world. If you are treated well by their staff, the odds of you quickly reporting to your networks about how great a time you are having, is **advertising they simply can't pay for.** Why? A testimonial from your friend is information you believe. If you are connected to that person online and see how much fun she is having, the Palms wins and it only cost them that bottle of champagne.

This is one of the best examples of online reputation catching up to real-world application that I've ever seen. Now you can expect to get checked by Starbucks, CoverGirl, Dannon Yogurt, Virgin America and Fox to name a few.

When I first heard about it, I didn't know whether to be upset or fascinated. I think it's a little of both. A friend asked me if I put any stock in Klout. I said that I didn't pay it much mind because the number seemed a little arbitrary. Also, they continue to alter their algorithms and my number swings wildly every couple of months.*

Then there's "those that talk about you." Many people are under the assumption that people talk more now than they did before the internet and mobile phones were around. We are social animals and we've been gossiping as long as we could form words, and probably before that (I have visions of grunting cavemen passing judgments upon each other's caves.).

The difference we are apt to notice is the ability for our words to travel farther and faster than ever before. I can talk negatively about you as my former friend or as a company I feel has wronged me. To really make it sting, I can share it with all the networks I belong to and have my words seen by hundreds or thousands of people in a relatively short period of time. **See Chapter 3: How to Deal with Negative Online Feedback**

*Excerpt from "Are You Cool Enough to Get Service? Klout Score Leads to Classism" published on my blog and available here: http://kerryregoconsulting.com/2010/10/02/are-you-cool-enough-to-get-service-klout-score-leads-to-classism/

~

WHAT'S THE WORST THAT COULD HAPPEN?

Maturity is something I don't see much of on social networks. So when it does appear, it's like a breath of fresh air.

A man I know is going through a tough time in his relationship. He confided to me that he had deactivated his Facebook account so that if his former partner decides to go off the rails, he's a little more protected.*

I say this almost every day: **nothing can be erased from the internet**. Not really. Once you tip over that box and the beans spill out, there is no recapturing it all. I hadn't yet had anyone tell me that they had proactively deactivated an account to protect themselves and I congratulated my friend on his foresight. Taking a pause while everyone cools off is a good idea.

The saying may be, "Sticks and stones may break my bones but words will never hurt me." In this case, they **can** hurt you.

[PSA Alert: Think of the horrible opportunities for "drunk dialing" that we can now be called "drunk posting." Don't post while under the influence!][23]

*Excerpt from "Don't Drink and Post" published on my blog and available here: http://kerryregoconsulting.com/2011/06/29/dont-drink-and-post/

There are so many ways that this can go wrong. An angry friend, colleague, or family member, can start a free blog in a matter of minutes (or use some other social tool) and slam you from here to Sunday. If you aren't paying attention, and don't have a presence online, they can damage your reputation beyond all recognition without you even knowing about it. **See Chapter 4: Strategy and Action Items**

A person doesn't even have to have malicious intent. A picture posted of you in your downtime by a friend or relative that is questionable or could be misinterpreted, can be disastrous (think about the parties you've been to or all the photos taken during holiday get-togethers). Your boss, potential boss, board, stockholders or the public may not like what they see. **Your job, livelihood, and reputation are at stake.** No one is going to watch out for you but you.

THE VIRAL NATURE OF
A SOCIAL MEDIA CRISIS

I'm pretty sure you've heard the term "it went viral." Often I hear it from a marketer who wants a YouTube video to be shared over and over and take on a life of its own and lead to untold riches. It's important for you to understand that, in my opinion, negative information spreads faster than fuzzy good news. You may have noticed this trend on televised news: you'll see a half-hour of bad stuff and one piece on a panda that gave birth at the zoo near the end of the newscast to end it on a light note. The proportions are in favor of negativity.

If your story goes viral, you must prepare yourself and your team for the worst-case scenario. I highly recommend having a Crisis Plan and running through it so that your team knows exactly what to do **when, not if,** a public relations crisis hits. **See Chapter 4: Legacy and Process Management**

An online crisis for a company can include unexpected website problems, lawsuits for data breaches, a staff member who goes off the rails and posts personal opinions (or worse) to the company Social Media channels, a disgruntled customer who has made it a personal mission to let the world know how bad your service is, or a truly defective product that has had hazardous results. How a crisis is handled online makes a massive difference to the future of the company.

Remember Toyota's brakes failing on a mass scale? Or the Deepwater Horizon British Petroleum oil spill contaminating the ocean for three months in 2010?

These are companies that truly had crises on their hands and had to work through it on a public stage. There isn't to say there wasn't a good reason for it, but BP suffered endless online parodies in the form of "memes" or viral picture jokes about the situation, videos, and constant online bashing all seen again and again by millions of people. Imagine trying to recover a reputation in the face of those odds.

~

CASE STUDY

In 2011, ChapStick created what they thought was a simple yet effective ad campaign. It featured a young woman hanging over the back of a couch, flinging cushions this way and that, with her backside in the air, desperately searching for her lost ChapStick. Apparently a blogger didn't care for the image and wrote about it. The blogger also commented about it on ChapStick's Facebook page where the catch line is "Be heard at Facebook.com/ChapStick." The company deleted the comments. Others objected as well and had their comments deleted. The comments landed fast and furious and the deleting continued. People began commenting on why their original comments had been deleted and ChapStick could no longer keep up with the deluge of angry traffic. During all of this, the original offending image stayed up, no apology was issued, and no mention of the company deleting of comments had happened. Finally, after recognizing it was a losing battle, ChapStick removed the image and issued this odd explanation with a quasi-apology wedged in:

> "We see that not everyone likes our new ad, and please know that we certainly didn't mean to offend anyone!" the post said. "Our fans and their voices are at the heart of our new advertising campaign, but we know we don't always get it right. We've removed the image and will share a newer ad with our fans soon!"

Here's the strange second paragraph:

> "We apologize that fans have felt like their posts are being deleted and while we never intend to pull anyone's comments off our wall, we do comply with Facebook guidelines and remove posts that use foul language, have repetitive messaging, those that are considered spam-like (multiple posts from a person within a short period of time) and are menacing to fans and employees."[24]

This is **not** how you want your brand to be remembered.

CHAPTER 3:

OBSTACLES, CONCERNS, AND SOLUTIONS

COMMON AREAS OF CONCERN

What are the common areas of concern around use of Reputation Management tools and Social Media? I've now heard them enough times that I can tell you right now what you are worried about.

- Public negativity
- Time required
- It's a waste of time
- Lack of staff
- Lack of training
- Fear of the unknown and mistakes
- Privacy and compliance
- Having multiple audiences
- We're B2B only

Public negativity

The short answer for this is, you can't hide from the world. It isn't perfect and people aren't always happy with you. Disgruntled customers and verbal detractors aren't a new phenomenon and they didn't sprout up because of the internet. You have already come to terms with what good customer service and effective communication are (I truly hope) and now you have to transfer those skills from three-dimensional space into the digital world. Many of the same techniques apply. You can't make it go away; it will only grow bigger.

I address this more deeply in two sections of this chapter with the subheadings **"How to deal with negative online feedback"** and **"Why deleting negative public posts is a bad idea."** This answer is so big, I really think you should skip ahead and read them.

Time required

The amount of time that's required to maintain a simple Social Media presence can be as little as a few minutes a day. If you are looking at having an aggressive presence, you'll need a strategy, focus, and more time (see **Chapter 4: Strategy and Action Items** for the strategy outline). But if you are simply monitoring your online reputation, a staff member may only need to devote a half hour a month. See **Chapter 4: How to get started in Reputation Management** for the tools you need to set up your routine.

It's really about a routine. Every company has procedures. On the first of the month you close your books, reconcile your accounting, do inventory and perform other similar tasks. Simply add reputation monitoring to the procedural list. As an individual, add it as a recurring appointment on your calendar to remind you.

The bottom line is, **no one has enough time**; that's the way time works. I don't have time to go to the dentist but I don't have a choice, I have to make the time. It really doesn't take as long as you fear it will, I promise. Your reputation is the only one you get so take good care of it.

It's a waste of time

Many decision makers are worried about employees spending time playing games, chatting with their friends, or whiling away valuable productive hours as they pretend to be working. Truthfully, if this is a concern for you, you have bigger staff time management problems than Social Media.

It can be viewed both ways. A Social Media campaign (and general internet use, for that matter) can be a huge time-suck or it can be seen as a huge productivity booster. It's a tool and how you use it determines the results you see.

With the return on investment calculation mentioned in **Chapter 2: How to Measure Return on Investment**, you can measure what benefits you are getting. The best way to keep the time investment to a minimum is to time yourself when working on tasks then tracking those efforts. **See Chapter 5: Metric Report**.

Lack of staff

Online Reputation Management and Social Media marketing are most commonly a function of the marketing department. Depending on the size of your company, you may not have a dedicated staff. If not marketing, it's an administrative task. With specific goals and objectives, a process list, and training, anyone can monitor a reputation and extend into marketing the business. Lack of time is the first side of this coin and not having the manpower to accomplish it is the other side. It doesn't require dedicated staff if you are simply monitoring your reputation. By placing these tasks in a list of procedures, the impact is minimal if even noticeable at all.

Lack of training

Anytime you make an investment in new equipment (or change procedure) you have to train your staff on how to deploy and use correctly. The same is true in digital concerns. You have a few different options.

- **YouTube:** Their number two category, behind music, is education. I've learned how to tie a toga and shuck an oyster using videos from YouTube, among other things. You can find a plethora of free information available at your fingertips at any hour of the day. The benefit is that it's free and the videos are in small, manageable chunks. The downside is that the videos may be out of date and might be inaccurate. When it comes to technology, you want the newest video on a subject because the tools continuously change and a video shot a year ago may give you instructions on a feature that doesn't exist or has vastly changed in the meantime. http://www.youtube.com

- **GCFLearnFree:** This is an amazing free online resource for training on digital tools, career, reading, math and more. It was created by the Goodwill Community Foundation International and has more content every time I look. http://www.gcflearnfree.org

- **Small Business Development Center or local college:** These are excellent physical resources where you can learn new tools or get help. The downside is their advanced offerings completely depend on your market and the teachers available. Most colleges are in the very early stages of offering classes in this niche.

- **City recreation and parks classes:** I have taught several classes in this realm and again it depends on your marketplace and the availability of teachers with the necessary skillset. This is a wonderfully affordable way to become comfortable with a new concept.

The other way to approach this is to **seek out professionals** such as myself. I'm not the only one out there but there are far fewer trainers than there are strategists. A technology or Social Media trainer will teach you and your staff to keep the tasks in-house, reducing the amount you will be spending month after month if you were to hire outside staff to manage your needs. This approach helps staff to take ownership over the process and outcome, and will empower your team to make smart decisions as the landscape changes. If they don't know what they are doing or how to do it, they are at a disadvantage, are dependent on others, and may feel compelled to outsource the function.

Meet with a trainer, set your goals, and build an in-house training program to keep your staff (and yourself) up-to-date and educated on the newest technology that are appropriate to your industry.

For individuals, you can take advantage of many of these same options. You won't have a need to create an in-house training program unless you believe your boss should consider such a thing. When it comes to hiring a professional such as myself, cost may be prohibitive. In this case, banding together with friends to create a custom group when hiring the professional is a great way to get the information you want and allows you to spread the cost to several people.

Fear

The fear of doing anything wrong can keep us from trying new foods, having new experiences, or going to new places. In digital media, the fear of making a costly mistake is real. When you don't know what you are doing and need help, seek out a professional to guide you through the process. Professionals can help you understand your needs, set goals, decide on tools, educate staff, set routines, and help you get up to speed. You can't know everything. Asking for help is a very important skill to have, and when it comes to the web, it's absolutely necessary. I do examine **Fear** in depth in the next section.

Privacy and compliance

We all need to keep confidential information about our clients private. That's normal. If other companies are using Social Media, they are finding a way to communicate without violating their clients' privacy. Let me tell you a story to show you how it's done. (For more on legal issues, please **see Chapter 3: Legal Implications.**)

I worked with a resort hotel in Sonoma County, CA several years ago. I built, upgraded, and managed the Facebook pages for four different departments while meeting with the managers once per month to help guide them with cross-departmental promotions. One of the divisions was doing wonderfully! They hit all the milestones a community manager wants to see for a Social Media platform: high levels of engagement from the users, independent conversation in the group without the need of a mediator, initiation of conversation, and use of multimedia content.

I completed my contract and not a month later, the best performing Facebook page was mistakenly deleted by an administrator. Poof, gone. I felt like I'd lost a child in traffic. I was no longer under contract and was simply asked what I thought they should do. I researched reinstating a deleted page and learned it took an average of two weeks to get it back. It could be done with patience and perseverance. They didn't listen to my advice and waited only one day before building a brand new page. I was so proud of what they had done and so sad to see all that history wiped out.

See? No privacy violation. You could guess what company it is but there are no identifying details. A majority of the content I either talk about in classes or post to my own Social Media channels is stripped of identifiers. You will learn to do the same with practice.

When it comes to compliance, the fields of legal, medical, insurance, and financial services do have compliance concerns and must have communications vetted by legal departments. It's all a part of routine. Educate yourself on what the requirements are for your industry, sit down once a week to write your blog or any other Social Media posts, and send them in for review. When it comes back to you approved, you are good to go. It just takes a little planning. These fields lose the immediacy of proactive communication but can still interact and "answer messages."

Many in these heavily restricted industries feel like their hands are tied when it comes to questions that can't be handled in the public eye. I like to think of this situation as a switchboard. The person asking will need to be redirected to the appropriate party and location. Here's an example for a doctor: a patient asks a question on a medical practice's Facebook page about a personal medical issue. The admin of the page is friendly when responding, "We'd love to help you with your needs. Please give your doctor a call today at 555-1212 to get a personalized answer." You **can** provide service with confidentiality in a public sphere.

Having multiple audiences

I've never worked with a company that had only one specific client. "But I do!" you say. Think really hard. Are all of your clients exactly the same? Is it possible that you have another audience? Or that they are using your product/service in multiple ways for a variety of end results? I'm willing to bet you do.

We all have to adapt our communication styles to fit different audiences that have differing needs. Know your audience and create mockups of who they are, what's important to them, and how to reach them. **See Chapter 4: Creating a Social Media strategy** for more detail.

To the organizations that assert they are B2B only (business to business), I say that the lines between B2B and B2C (business to consumer) have been blurred. There are certain industries that won't be talking to their customers on a tool such as Facebook or YouTube. But you must remember that we aren't separated from information by B2B or B2C classifications when using the internet. Decision makers for purchasing are also consumers and they **do** interact with B2C tools in their personal and professional lives. If your reputation stinks or their friends are trashing you on one of those sites, do you think they won't pay attention?

~

FEAR

The longer I work with people, the more I realize we are all the same and want the same things in life. I've learned that we are all afraid. Everyone. I'm talking to you right now. You get scared at little things and big things alike. And I'm telling you that everyone else does too. You aren't deficient, unworthy, or different.

Everyone is scared.

Let's get specific about the fear of technology. Technophobia is the fear or dislike of advanced technology or complex devices, especially computers.[25] I remember learning about machines as a child, the most basic being the lever. Think how long we've had new-fangled technology in our midst; technology has always given us grief and caused trepidation, and computers aren't the first to have this effect on us. The workers of the Industrial Revolution were among the first to experience displacement due to technological advances. Many of them sabotaged machines in an attempt to slow (or derail) the pace of adoption. Clearly, they were not successful.

Here are common refrains I hear from people of all walks of life:

- I'm too old to learn how to use a computer
- I didn't grow up with computers like young people today
- My clients don't use computers so I don't need to either
- I have some sort of weird electrical current that flows through my body and I disrupt the normal functions of computers (I hear this one more than you'd believe!)
- It's all too much
- I don't have the time
- I'm afraid I'll break it
- I should know this; everyone else does
- I'm stupid

What I know now is that fear is underneath every one of those statements. I'm not saying that how you feel isn't valid but it's stopping you from doing many things in your life and the need to be comfortable with technology is inescapable.

I gave an O'Reilly Ignite talk on this subject that you can watch here: http://bit.ly/IgniteFear

I'm too old to learn how to use a computer

You are only as old as you feel. You learn new things every single day. There is no age limit as to when you stop learning. The largest growing group for social network use is 74 years old and older, according to Pew Research Center's 2011 study. Their use has quadrupled from 2008 to 2011.[26] As of August 2011, 86 percent of internet users over 65 use email, 48 percent use it on an average day.[27] If my 91-year old grandmother can do it, so can you.

I didn't grow up with computers like you did

At what age did you learn to walk, tie your shoes, or balance your checkbook? Think about the job you are in now. Did you learn to do that at a young age? Maybe you did, but I know you can think of several things you do today that you didn't learn how to do until you were an adult.

Many people think computer use is generational. I have to tell you that younger people aren't smarter (clearly) but they've been exposed to technology longer so they may **seem** smarter when it comes to the subject. The truth of it is they are simply more comfortable. If you've read the book *Outliers* by Malcolm Gladwell, you are familiar with the concept of being an expert. In his opinion, if you have 10,000 hours of experience at something, you are an expert. It boils down to practice. Anyone can master something, or become adept, with enough practice. Trust me, it gets easier.

My clients don't use computers so I don't need to

Remember when I talked about what's happening to the phone book? Well, your customers are using computers in a wide variety of ways: cell phones, ATM machines, kiosks, laptops, Kindles, and electric cars. Heck, even farmers out in the fields are on the ball. They are using mobile applications to help them take soil readings, global positioning system sensors to track seed populations, and use wifi credit card readers to take payments at farmers markets. A 2011 study by the American Farm Bureau Federation revealed that of the 98 percent of farmers and ranchers ages 18 to 25 who have internet access, 76 percent of them use social media.[28]

I have some kind of electrical current that disrupts machines (also known as "I make machines go kerfluey")

You'd be surprised how frequently I hear this one. For the first few years, I gave them the benefit of the doubt. But now I've heard it so many times, I don't think that it's your body. I think this can be solved with a positive attitude. Coming from someone who uses computers all day long, sometimes stuff doesn't work. Often the site you are using is experiencing difficulties, your internet connection is spotty, your computer needs to be shut down, you haven't been updating your machine regularly (yes, those updates are actually necessary), or your browser is out of date (please don't use Internet Explorer if you can help it). When you call traditional technical support, the first thing they tell you to do is make sure your power source is plugged in. Most of my issues are solved by properly turning off the machine and then back on again. Really.

It's all too much

I agree. I feel overwhelmed as well. But you can turn it off and walk away when that happens. Take a break when you need to. New challenges are just that, challenges. But you face obstacles that you must overcome every day.

But let's return to the generational assumption that younger people are better at adapting to technology than you or like it more. I find many younger people are just as overwhelmed and are also trying to dial it back. In a study by Common Sense Media, 36 percent of teens who responded wish "they could go back to a time when there was no Facebook."[29]

One way to combat this is to turn off the dingers, ringers, buzzers, and notifications. Take a sabbatical on a regular basis from all the equipment. I try very hard not to use any electronics in my bedroom. The light disturbs your brainwaves and makes it very difficult to shut down. National Sleep Foundation, "The higher use of these potentially more sleep-disruptive technologies (computers, laptops, tablets, cell phones, and televisions) among younger generations may have serious consequences for physical health, cognitive development and other measures of wellbeing."[30] Other generations are not excluded from this finding. Along with health experts, I recommend not using these kinds of devices for at least an hour before you go to bed.

I discovered a secret – **the antidote to technology is Nature.**[31] We are stressed out. We are tired. We are sick. But it doesn't have to be that way. Talk a walk. Play more. Eat fresh food. Dig in the dirt. Watch or swim in natural water. Listen carefully to your body and the world around you. The solution to this problem has no batteries.

Surprised to hear that coming from me? That last paragraph is an excerpt from a blog I wrote on the subject and I think it's important. I encourage you learn more about how I reached that conclusion and read it here: http://kerryregoconsulting.com/2012/04/29/the-antidote-to-technology/

I don't have the time

My answer to this lament is that I don't have time to go to the gym or get my oil changed but I don't have a choice in the matter. I have to **make** the time. It's up to you to determine how much time is necessary to accomplish the task you have in front of you. We often assume it will take much longer than what the reality ends up being. Set a timer and it makes you move faster. I say, work like you're on fire.

I'm afraid I'll break it

This one is understandable. We think of computers and other tech as delicate and easy to damage. No, it won't explode. No, it won't go up in smoke. It's much harder than you think to completely destroy a computer. Most likely your fear is really about making a mistake. We make mistakes all the time. Say it with me, "Oops!" Practice that one a little every day and you get better at it. (C'mon! Give it a try.)

You know what computers have that most things in life don't? It's called "Undo." It's brilliant! If you were to spend a few hours in my office with me on any given day, you'd hear me say several times, "Oh no! Undo, undo, undo." And like magic, it fixes your mistake. The thing you have to do is remind yourself is that the function exists. It's in your web browser (including Internet Explorer, Firefox, Chrome, Opera, and Safari) and in many of your software programs and suites including Microsoft Office. If you use a PC mouse, the right-click button has a little menu. Depending on what you are doing or which program you are using, an Undo option often appears on that menu as well. On the toolbar it usually looks like an arrow that bends to the left.

Computer manufacturers make it quite difficult for you to break your machine. I've been using computers for 30 years and training others for 18. I've never seen someone actually break a machine.

I should know this; everyone else does

No they don't. And why **should** you know this stuff? So much of it is new and it wasn't in the curriculum when you were in school (they barely teach it today but that's another, much longer story). You think everyone else around you knows what you don't. Guess what? Most people are faking it. Or they think they know and they really don't. We are wired to "fake it until we make it." The smartest people in the world don't know everything, they know how to ask questions. The trick is to ask help of the right person or someone who can help you get closer to the answer. The only way to learn more is to ask!!!

I'm stupid

This one makes me really sad. I work with CEOs, managing directors, doctors, lawyers, teachers, seniors, moms, dads, kids, and students. I hear this almost every day from people in every category, no matter their age. I just want to hold their hand when they say this. Sometimes I do.

If this is how you feel, please know that you are entirely capable of learning new things. You do it every day! I'm going to pull rank as a professional tech trainer here. Listen to me when I say you **CAN** learn. You **CAN** conquer new challenges. You **ARE** capable. Let me be the voice in your head telling you that you **CAN DO IT.**

Don't let your fears derail you from opportunities.

~

OUR NEEDS

I want to talk about the hierarchy of human needs by American psychologist Abraham Maslow. It's a theory from his 1943 paper "A Theory of Human Motivation"[32] and I want to look at it in relation to fear. Take a look at the diagram and we'll familiarize ourselves with a visualization of the importance of our human needs.

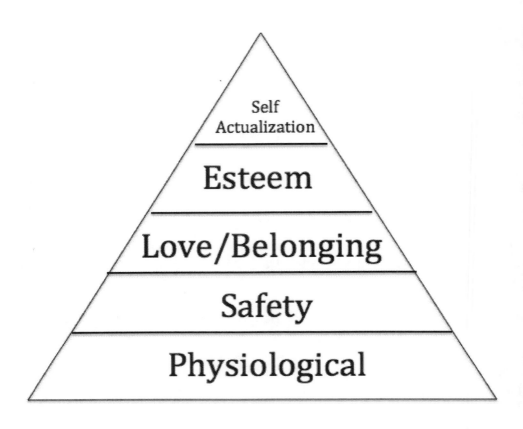

- The bottom rung is **Physiological** needs such as: breathing, food, water, sex, sleep, etc.

- The second is where it starts to apply to the fear of computers, and I promise I'll make the connection for you shortly. Second is **Safety,** such as security of: body, employment, resources, family, health, and property.

- Third is **Love/belonging** and it covers: friendship, family, sexual intimacy.

- Fourth is **Esteem** and it covers: self-esteem, confidence, achievement, respect of others, and respect by others.

- And last is **Self-Actualization**: morality, creativity, spontaneity, problem solving, lack of prejudice, and acceptance of facts.

Not understanding how to use a computer, whether it's a desktop, laptop, netbook, tablet, mobile device, ATM machine, electric vehicle, or other, directly fits into three of the categories of needs.

Safety

Security of employment is the biggest here. Do you have job security? Will enhanced technological ability increase your value? Many people who are at risk of losing their jobs today wouldn't be able to compete in the job market because they lack many of the basic computer skills required in the classifieds or on job listing sites on the web. Now that paper newspapers are on the decline, you need to know your way around a computer to search for a job as well as apply for one. This need fulfillment is **at risk**.

Love/belonging

When everyone around you is using some kind of mobile device, you can easily be left out. From instant messaging and texting conversations to your kids sharing pictures of your grandkids on Facebook, you can easily be left out of the communication loop if you aren't online. Even when people are talking face-to-face today, so much of the conversation revolves around something they saw, said, or shared on a Social Media channel. Your sense of belonging is **at risk**.

Esteem

Again, everyone around you is obsessively using devices of all kinds. It's not that you want to use them or that you should be using them. The fact that the majority of your friends, family, and co-workers are using technology constantly (holidays, dinner outings, everywhere you go) means you are left out of belonging to the larger group and your esteem suffers. If you don't know how to use them, you are deeper in this hole. Your esteem is **at risk**.

Check In

Are you feeling a little panicky? I'm probably stoking your fears. My goal is not to make you feel bad, but I need to demonstrate that your desire to not use computers is starting to threaten your security in a variety of ways.

You may throw down this book right now and say, "Kerry is trading on fear! I don't need this. I disagree." That's okay if that's how you feel. I hope that doesn't happen. If you do set the book down, I hope it's to ponder these ideas and to explore your reactions.

I will now return to the concept I stated earlier that we are all the same and want the same things. It boils down to love. We all want to be loved and accepted. You can see it right there in Maslow's diagram. We really do. When you strip away cars, money, success, college degrees, and the façade we put up, we all need the same things.

Truthfully, I am concerned about every demographic I can think of in relation to lack of tech knowledge. The group I'm most worried about is the successful decision maker, or The Boss. Why would I worry about The Boss? For many years I was a personal and executive assistant and I worked with business owners, executives, some millionaires, and a few celebrities. I noticed that they become very isolated, rely on others for the smallest tasks, and often feel unable to show vulnerability due to their increased status.

They have people make phone calls for them, obtain information, control their finances, shop, cook, and send emails; it goes on and on. **Imagine not knowing** how to make a phone call, drive a car, make reservations at a restaurant, or shop for yourself. All of these functions are largely automated using the internet or some other computerized technique. Where do people in this situation go to learn how to do some of the most basic daily tasks? They don't. They rarely have the opportunity to show that they are out of the loop and need help, or their ego may prevent them from seeking out information. It can be seen as a sign of weakness that people can be intelligent, possibly wealthy, and a force to be reckoned with in their field, but still not know how to use their smartphone or send email. See how this is a dangerous place to be? I worry about The Boss because she can be trapped without a lifeline. I see a lot of these people behind closed doors but I know

I'm not reaching even a fraction of them. You might not be The Boss but everyone has the need to be self-reliant.

Change is the one thing you can depend on every single day.

Here are steps to deal with change:

- **Accept that it will happen**. If you fight it, life can be a painful experience.
- **Educate yourself**. We fear what we don't know. Write down the questions or concerns you have, then find the information that will help you understand.
- **Focus**. It's so easy to become distracted and overwhelmed. Keep a tight focus on what you are trying to accomplish by breaking down a large problem into smaller pieces. If you take one bite of the elephant at a time, it doesn't seem like such a large animal.
- **Set time limits for yourself**. I love the timer on my phone and stove. Any task I don't want to do, I set the timer so I know that the buzzer will sound soon and release me or remind me not to get too wrapped up.
- **Be patient**. My little girl gets so frustrated with herself when she tries something for the first time and doesn't master it immediately. You're probably no different. Every person who became good at something needed to put in a lot of practice. Computers are kinetic and require muscle memory. You will need to do it again and again before your body and brain remember how and it becomes more natural.

Take a deep breath, step into it, and you'll be okay.

If you missed it the first time, I gave an O'Reilly Ignite talk on this subject that you can watch here: http://bit.ly/IgniteFear

~

LEGAL IMPLICATIONS

I sit on a committee that allows me to interact with a wide variety of civil servants and government departments. I'm there as a web geek to offer technical information and advice. Our conversations range from return on investment (ROI) of Social Media to technical use and policy enforcement.

In one of those meetings, I heard an update from a member of law enforcement about a software demo he had received from a vendor. It was with one of the most noted and widely respected media engagement and monitoring software tools available. The vendor mentioned it had been developed for the corporate world, but it had promising applications for law enforcement. Examples of searches they could perform included: gang activity, specific gang names, graffiti tagging, bomb making, and stolen property, to name a few. All the information came from public sources such as Twitter and Facebook posts. The tool simply sped up the process of discovering needles in a haystack. Police officers were able to see gang members posting photos of tags and read conversations about them claiming their work and territory as well as threatening others. Detectives can upload manifests of stolen property and find the items listed on sites that sell goods, such as Craigslist. One of the search demos had accidentally uncovered a plot by students to bring pipe bombs to school.

This shows that law enforcement is actively finding ways to take advantage of Social Media and that these tools are becoming standard practice for investigations. I imagine that very soon, police departments will commonly have a staff position for Social Media investigations and data mining. Officers themselves are going to have this in their skill sets.

In 2011, the International Association of Chiefs of Police conducted a survey of 800 law enforcement agencies and discovered that nearly nine out of ten use some form of Social Media. More than 50 percent report that these tools have helped to solve crimes.[33] One of my favorite examples of law enforcement use of new tools is a picture of New York Police Department (NYPD) Police Commissioner Ray Kelly and Jack Dorsey, CEO of Twitter, at the NYPD command center in front of a wall of monitors that show a live feed of Twitter in the background.[34] The officers use it to help them "listen" to what's happening in the city.

Your behavior online can affect you and what you post online is fair game. If you say it out loud outside of your own home, law enforcement may very well witness what you do. I hear about many people with an expectation of privacy when communicating on the internet. This is a false expectation and there is no longer privacy as we used to know it.

Don't forget that your employment contract may stipulate you not reveal trade secrets, propriety information, engage in harassing behavior, or discuss others' state of employment. You may be fired or sued based on the information you share.

~

INTELLECTUAL PROPERTY VIOLATIONS

Remember the boombox; you know, the radio/cassette tape player that allowed you to record music either off the radio or from another tape? Copying someone else's property is illegal and we know that. Most of us weren't selling bootlegged tapes, we were making mixes to give to our friends. It seemed fairly innocent at the time so everyone looked the other way. No one sued Sony or Phillips for including the record button on those machines.

When computers grew to be common, burning CDs, downloading from Napster, and making playlists became really easy. All of a sudden it was a true threat to musicians and recording companies. That's when the lawsuits started.

If you are an artist and you put your heart, sweat, and tears into a piece of art, it's your intellectual property and is protected by law*. Unfortunately, this important detail isn't being taught to computer users. The nature of Social Media is to share with others. So, if it's illegal to share other people's content, then why are we allowed to do it? I didn't say it made sense. Just because it's easy to steal, doesn't make it right.

Some owners of vast libraries of intellectual property use firms to hunt down their content when it's used fraudulently, such as The Beatles or Joni Mitchell, and they will sue you. You will first receive a cease and desist letter before further legal action is taken. If your use of their content is in violation of the law that may not be the only legal action you see.

It's important to understand that legally, you can only share what is yours and which you own the copyright. Look at the terms of use for all the major social networks. They are all similar. The website is protected and you are not. Pinterest, a site that allows you to easily post and share photos that you own or that you have found almost anywhere on the web, is a big driver of the conversation around this issue which has yet to be handled or completely understood. The copyright laws we currently have on the books were written before digital media was even a twinkle in our eye, as they say. The laws don't address the issues that these new forms of media and sharing present us with though this landscape is changing daily with ongoing proposals for new laws.

My recommendation to you is that if you have a website, write a blog, run any Social Media channels, or share content in any way, make sure you are using your own words, images, and video. Most people don't think of it as stealing but look at it through the eyes of the copyright holder and the law. Ensure the content you use is that which you have the right to post.

When I say this information in a presentation or class I'm giving, there's always one person who says he looks up an image on the internet, gets a satisfactory result (usually from Google Images), and then puts the image on his blog/Facebook/Pinterest site. The look of realization on the person's face when it hits him that it's not okay is crushing to watch.

Hire a photographer, copywriter, or videographer to create content for you if you don't feel you can do it yourself. Sign a contract that stipulates your usage and ownership of that content and negotiate full rights. Make a list of the type of photos (or other content) you'll need for a variety of marketing communications and set up your own photo shoot. If you have someone on your team with the skill to do it, you can use smartphones or other inexpensive digital equipment to ensure your legal security in this area.

*I am not a lawyer and am not implying that I have full understanding of the law. Please talk to an attorney about any concerns you may have about your rights or possible violations. If you need a lawyer that specializes in technology, please contact me for a referral.

~

WHY YOU MUST HAVE A COMMUNICATIONS POLICY

My clients often ask me about Social Media policies and how they go about obtaining one. In response, I ask if they have a communications policy. If you own or manage a business, you have some kind of employee manual. Take a look at the table of contents and find where communication fits in. Most likely you have some kind of procedure regarding how you interface with colleagues and the public. This is the natural place for Social Media and new media to fit in. If you were to write a separate policy specific to Facebook or Twitter, as an example, it would be too narrow of an approach. Tomorrow a new tool could be introduced that will force you to rewrite the whole Social Media policy. This will happen again and again. On a regular basis, your manual and procedures should be reviewed for accuracy related to current use. **See Chapter 4: Legacy and Process Management**

I hope that you see these new tools as opportunities. If your procedural manual has a section that addresses phone or written communication, then maybe a section just for Social Media (and every other form) makes sense.

Generally, all forms are lumped together: phone, fax, written, email, web, face-to-face. Social Media gets added to the list. I do suggest you address it in the regard to editorial approval process, what constitutes appropriate and inappropriate content, and what to do in a public relations crisis situation.

Don't single it out and treat it differently because it's not that distant from what you are already using. Again, any time you create a new policy or rule, you must communicate with staff as to how it affects them and train for those changes. I call it Social Media sensitivity training.

~

HOW TO DEAL WITH NEGATIVE ONLINE FEEDBACK

When asked about negative online comments I say, "Any company that has been in business longer than five minutes has an unhappy customer. You simply can't please everyone all the time." How you deal with it is more telling than the fact that the negativity exists. The lack of control over what people say about businesses makes many owners uncomfortable. I'll let you in on a secret: **the internet didn't take away your control. You never had control.**

Control is only an illusion. The only thing you actually control in any situation is how you react.

According to the Opinion Research Corporation, 84 percent of Americans say online reviews influence their purchasing decisions so this is an important area to monitor. I was doing a Reputation Management platform audit for one of my clients, a bike and kayak touring company, when I came across a negative review on Trip Advisor. The customer was displeased with the tour he received and felt it wasn't what he expected during purchase. The owner dealt with it in an effective way. He apologized, told the customer that the next tour was on him, and that he'd take the customer out himself. Done. It was a negative turned into a positive, at least from my perspective.

You can learn a lot about a person/business from the way they treat people. The owner handled it the way he would have if the client had been standing in his place of business. The way we cope with online feedback should be similar to the way we'd handle it face-to-face. You use the same skills but in a new "location." The additional benefit of handling online negativity well is it lends transparency to your process. Others can see what happened, how you handle business, and can make their own conclusions about the service you provide.

Let's talk about having your friends or employees write reviews for you. It's called astroturfing. Astroturfing[35] is a bogus grass roots movement or the practice of disingenuously creating reviews for a service that come from someone other than an actual customer. Lifestyle Life, a cosmetic surgery clinic in New York, was required to pay $30,000 in civil penalties after an investigation by the state attorney general's office. Employees had been found guilty of posing as plastic surgery patients and had been writing wonderful reviews. It's tempting. Don't do it. Also, don't promise free merchandise or services for good reviews. You are in effect paying for their words. It's the same premise with a different approach.

Good tech support can help prevent bad reviews. 45 percent of retail customers prefer social media support, according to ZenDesk. Do you know what kind of support your customers prefer? Give them a survey, high tech or low tech. The important part is to know their preference before it gets to the bad review stage.

Ways to prevent negativity*

- **Listen constantly.** Make sure you are aware of what your customers are saying every day of the week. If you are afraid of what you'll find, you are simply sticking your head in the sand and this could be the end of you. Make sure what you hear is accurate; if it isn't, open a line of dialogue to make a correction–not an argument but a correction. Bad reviews can highlight where larger issues are hiding.

- **Acknowledge the complaint.** We all want to be heard and seen. Being polite goes a long way. Sometimes you will hear from people that have very few other things going on in their life and your kind response can diffuse a situation that if ignored, could spiral out of control.
- **Fix it fast.** Your audience is intoxicated with the power they now have to build up or destroy your reputation quickly. Make sure everyone in the company knows to treat each client, caller, and any person they come in contact with, as if that person is the most important client the company has. Manage their expectations about timeframe of resolution.
- **Take it offline.** Offer to communicate with them in a more private setting such as email or over the phone so that you can take it off the public stage.
- **Be honest.** Care about your customers, engage when they want to hear from you, and offer to fix any problems. Provide great customer service.

*Remember, you can't completely prevent all negativity. Sometimes people are cranky and take it out on the wrong person. As misguided as it is, there are people that have limited human contact and picking a fight online satisfies that need for them. Also, there are unbalanced people out there or those with unresolved anger issues. If you know you handled the person with respect, your public can see that and will be able to differentiate a true service request from an unreasonable communication. If you have a harassment situation on your hands, each one of the Social Media platforms has recourse for reporting and protection.

Let's say you really did mess up.

Apologize

This can be hard for people, but sometimes the complainer just wants to be validated or acknowledged. If a customer complains about a pizza arriving late, the company should respond with an apology and might promise a free item on the next order. Tracking complaints will allow you to spot recurring issues. This accomplishes several things: the customers are happier because they've been acknowledged, you are tracking a possible problem in your service chain, and the general public can witness how you handled the situation.

Procedure

When a simple apology won't solve the situation, you need to have a more organized approach. Have a dedicated contact person who can take ownership over issues and see them through to resolution. Having someone responsible for tracking complaints will allow you to see a larger service problem, should that be the case.

- **Set expectations for the customer.** After the initial contact with the customer, let her know when a full response will be forthcoming. If the complaint is in a public arena, strive to take it private as soon as possible. It will be easier on the customer and keeps further negativity out of the public eye. Time isn't your friend if the complaint originated online. Find a resolution fast.
- **Publicly respond with the resolution.** This could be an explanation or maybe a discount. This is your call as your business model is yours and yours alone. If it started in a public forum, make sure you let the public know that you care about customer service issues and that you work hard to make it right. If it began on Twitter, post your public resolution there.
- **Make changes where necessary.** By having your process in place you will be able to make necessary changes to the way you deliver your product and improve the customer experience.
- **Encourage your Super Fans.** These are the greatest cheerleaders for your brand. Their opinion about what you do is worth more than any advertising. Their amplification of positive opinions is priceless.
- **Don't take it personally.** Unhappy customers happen. It's part of being in business. You need to make sure you did everything you needed to do at the end of the day.

The only thing you truly control is how you respond to a situation.

It's how you react to a situation that the public remembers. By taking a potentially horrible incident and turning it around with great customer service, you can wipe away a bad experience and earn new customers with the way you respond.

An army of empowered consumers is defining your brand for you. Make sure you are involved.

~

WHY DELETING NEGATIVE PUBLIC POSTS IS A BAD IDEA

I know it's tempting, but it's considered bad form to delete a post from one of your online channels just because you don't like what that person has to say. As business owners, we have to come to terms with the fact that the second we open our "doors," someone somewhere is unhappy. We can't please everyone all of the time. Now, the whole purpose of using Social Media is to have conversations and communicate with others. If you are a page administrator who removes a post by the public simply because the content isn't what you prefer, then you don't understand what Social Media is really about.

I recommend deleting and removing posts from others if they are: racist, sexist, full of hate speech, obscene or violate your stated community guidelines. Deleting simply because you don't like it shows immaturity and an inability to deal with real life situations. No matter how much you try to whitewash life, you can't remove all negativity from the world. Instead of pulling out the big pink eraser, acknowledge the concern (if the person isn't delusional), communicate with the person, validate the concern, then discuss your plan of action, whatever it is. Remember, there is always someone watching your actions and there are silent members of your audience who **will** notice.[36] Transparency wins.

The way you deal with unhappy or negative people is proof of your character. A less-than-rosy comment doesn't have to be the end of the world.

It can be a learning experience if you are open to it. Have you ever had cruddy customer service, complained, then received excellent treatment and it changed the way you thought of the company? It happens to me all the time. People love to bag on telephone reps. I love it when I get a truly helpful and nice person. It happens more often than people acknowledge but sometimes it's the way Ginny from Oklahoma treats you that determines how you feel about the multi-billion dollar corporation. Take every opportunity as a chance to provide a stellar experience. It's never too late to turn it around!

Bottom line? Deleting posts damages your credibility. It can also further anger the original commenter (**see Chapter 2: Case study ChapStick**).

*Excerpt from "Be Transparent: Why Deleting Negative Posts is a Bad Idea" published on my blog and available here: http://kerryregoconsulting.com/2012/06/22/be-transparent-why-deleting-negative-posts-is-a-bad-idea/

~

CHARACTER ALWAYS WINS

You've heard the saying, "A lady never _____." No one ever said this to me directly but I did take note of class all by myself. I don't live in a world where gloves, pearls, and finger sandwiches exist but the pearls are still the sign of a classy lady.

There is an image of this lady in my head. Sometimes she looks like Audrey Hepburn, quiet and graceful with doe eyes. Other times she is Claire Huxtable from the Cosby Show. She is a smart, clever, funny, beautiful woman who does not suffer fools.

When I am approached about my thoughts on privacy issues and the internet, the ghost of that lady is in my head. When Google Buzz unintentionally released users' address books to all of the individuals whose names were within those address books, the ensuing uproar over loss of privacy and security was expected. I heard somewhere that it's really about control. We were under the illusion that we had control over our information. When we lose that control, we get upset. But the question I want to ask is, did we ever really have control?

I say this, "From the second you step out your door, you are most likely being recorded. Your activities are being recorded by the security cameras in your complex, the passing Google Street View car, a satellite image, a cell phone with camera and video, the computers you use, the emails and texts you send, and the credit cards you charge with-pretty much everything you do is being tracked. You can't let that stop you from living your life, but I hope you think twice about the choices you make."

When on Facebook, I am reminded that my grandmother, stepmom, sister and clients are reading my posts and seeing my activity. I am telling you, there is nothing like a grandma watching to keep you in line. (If yours isn't online or isn't a social networking buddy, posting a photo of her near your computer does just as well.)

I recently passed what I call "The Lady Test." A woman I respect for her honesty, intelligence, wit, devotion, and genteel nature expressed to me how impressed she was with the way I carried myself, who I was, and how I conducted business. This is a woman that definitely fits into the lady category. It doesn't matter that she is younger than I am. To know that those I esteem recognize in me those same qualities means I am making the right choices.

Can you pass the "lady test"? You don't have to be a woman. It's about conducting yourself in a certain way, a way that makes you or your family proud. Know that everything you do counts and that every person you come in contact with is affected by you. There are no throw-aways or do-overs. Pretend your grandma's watching.[37]

*Originally published as "The Lady Test: Privacy, Decorum and Online Behavior" on my blog and is available here:
http://kerryregoconsulting.com/2010/08/13/the-lady-test-privacy-decorum-and-online-behavior/

CHAPTER 4:

STRATEGY AND ACTION ITEMS

HOW TO GET STARTED
IN REPUTATION MANAGEMENT

I hope you read some of the information leading up to this section to have a better feel for the importance of protecting your online reputation. If you skipped right to this part, that's okay too.

Why can't you simply pay someone to do this for you? You can sign up for services at websites such as Reputation Defender, Remove Your Name, and Integrity Defenders to help but they really only do two things. One, they will request on your behalf that negative information about you or your company be taken down. Two, they will help you create new content to displace negative content. They can't guarantee removal of negative content; they can only ask on your behalf. Some of the sites that have your information incorrect may not even be in business anymore. Many websites run automatically because their domains are prepaid or they are scraping information from another site. Sending out hundreds of requests may not get you very far. And you will end up paying a lot of money for those services on a monthly or package basis. When I say a lot of money, I mean it.

The recommendations here are free except for the time it takes (and the cost of this book!). By doing it yourself, you will have more ownership over the process. I think this is preferable to depending on a company that may or may not be in business next year to do it for you. Remember, Reputation Management is ongoing so it's an expense you'll have to continue to meet if you don't set up your own process to do it.

I want to manage your expectations around the action plan I'm about to lay out for you. **You will not be able to accomplish all of this in one day**. You will want to set aside time to accomplish these tasks on a regular basis (maybe once or twice a week) until you've worked your way through the list. Pace yourself. What you learn about the online image of your name and your business during this process will be worth the effort.

Let's get started.

~

ACTION ITEMS

Perform a vanity search

This is most commonly called "Google-ing yourself". Enter your name, business name, or "known as" names into search engines. Make sure you do this on not just Google, but Bing, Yahoo!, Blekko, and any other search tool you prefer. Just because Google-powered search engines have 68 percent market share[38] doesn't mean they are the only player whose search results merit attention. According to the website (and Reputation Management service) Brand Yourself, 94 percent of people check only the first page of search results. I recommend not stopping there. Go as far into those search results as you can. Don't give up until you stop seeing results associated with you. Dig like your professional life depends on it. It just might.

- Navigate to http://www.google.com (or http://www.yahoo.com or http://www.bing.com or other). Google is considered the most popular search engine so it's best to start there. You can expand to others for somewhat different results. Make sure that if you have a Google account, you've logged out before you start your search. This will give you unbiased results. In the future, your computer's unique identifying number will be recognized by search engines so you will need to use a different computer for what they call "virgin results".
- Type your name or business name into the search bar. Put your name between quotation marks for more accurate results, such as "John H. Smith."
- Scroll through the results and click on each one to see what the website is or what it says about you. Often it's about another person all together.
- Write down anything you want to follow up on, positive or negative, or print the pages. Make notes about incorrect information.

- If you're not finding much on you, expand your original search by adding keywords related to your location, employer, industry, and schools.

Setup Google Alerts

Now that you've done a manual search for where you and your name stand, you can set up an automated service to do it on a more frequent basis.

A word about Google Accounts…

Many of the tools I mention in this section are services available to you with a Google account. You can have a free account or upgrade and use their Business Solutions/Google Apps for Business. Every Google tool I talk about in this book is based on the use of a free account. I do recommend that you get yourself one account to link all the services you use together under one "roof". You don't need to have a Gmail address (the email service Google offers) to have this account. It can be started with any email address. **Be warned: it is extremely difficult or even impossible at the time this book was written to switch some services from one Google account to another.** Set up a general Google account that isn't assigned to any one person, if possible. I have seen companies where all of their services go away with the employee that just left because the services were linked to their personal account. Put a lot of thought into the setup of the account before you open it.

Back to our regularly scheduled programming.

Let's get you set up with an automated web search by using Google Alerts. You don't have to worry about what could be appearing online in your personal or business name because alerts monitor the web for you. You can get emails sent to the email address associated to your Google account that cover: what's being said about your company or product, a developing news story, a competitor or industry, or the latest news on any subject. I like using it creatively to monitor posts about a physical event such as a conference.

- Log into your Google account
- Navigate to http://www.google.com/alerts
- Type into the Search Query box the term you'd like monitored. This could be your name, industry, event, or others.
- Click on the arrow next to Result Type. I choose Everything but you can make your own decision on this.
- Click on the arrow to select How Often you want your results. If you are in the middle of a public relations crisis, choose As It Happens but if not, go with Once a Day.
- How Many? I say, All Results.
- Deliver to your email associated with the account or you can send it to an RSS feed.
- Create the Alert.
- Or you can click on Manage Your Alerts to edit and view what you already have.

Once you start receiving alerts, you can create, edit, or delete right out of the emails. You can use other alert systems such as Yahoo! Alerts, Social Mention, or Brand Yourself. They all function similarly. Brand Yourself starts free but offers upgrade options. It will also give you action items to improve your results.

.com

Own your own domain

Buy your name, variations, misspellings, and business name(s), if you can. You can have them redirect to any website you like. I own KerryRego.com and it points to KerryRegoConsulting.com. I recommend a .com first and .net second.

Go to http://www.godaddy.com, http://www.domain.com, or some other domain purchasing service and buy your domain name. Domain names generally run anywhere from $3 to $10 per year with a price break if you buy multiple years or domains at a time. If you are planning on using it to create content rather than simply owning it, purchase more than one year at a time. Search engines can see that you've purchased multiple years and know that you are in business for the long haul. It's a ranking factor that pushes you up higher in search results.

The email address you assign to the account when you purchase it should be one you use and check regularly. You will receive a notification from the company when the domain is getting close to expiration. When it expires, it goes back onto the open market and it's gone. You may be able to get it back but it'll cost you. A web designer I know said it cost him $150 to get a domain back. Be responsible when you change email boxes and don't close down the old one right away, if you can. Lots of straggler emails come in over time and you can update old accounts with new information. You can also set your domains up on auto renewal. The problem with that is your credit cards have expiration dates as well. Between the two steps, you should be able to make sure they never expire without your knowledge.

I know that some industry competitors buy the names, business names, and all keyword domains associated with their industry. I've even heard of some buying the actual name of their competition. I can only imagine the realization (then anger) on the part of the business that discovers that they don't own their own name because **their direct competitor does.**

If you have children, buy their domain names for them **right now**. It is an investment that is worth far more than the pennies you will spend on securing their digital real estate for their future. When they are ready to apply for college or get a job, their domain can be pointed to any number of free websites they can build themselves like Google Sites or a Wordpress blog. They will be able to showcase their schoolwork, community service, or other points of pride. You can share with them that they **will** be checked out by their future employer or school counselor.

Buying a domain in multiple year blocks isn't as important for your child's name as when you are trying to build an online business reputation. You can buy one year at a time to keep more money in your pocket. You may choose to buy as many years as possible so that you don't have to think about it. The risk with that is that you might forget about the domain because you purchased it so long ago and the email assigned to the account will likely get closed over that extended time period. I like one year at a time for this need.

When it's time to hand over the reins, simply call the customer service number on the website (this is why I like GoDaddy, their customer service rocks) and they will walk you through the process of redirecting or switching ownership to your now adult child.

True story: I have a friend that is a Broadway performer and she didn't buy her own domain before someone else did. When one does a search for her name a XXX performer comes up before her. I know at least one other person that has this same problem. Own your own name before someone else buys it.

Another thing to consider when you own your own domain is to use the email addresses associated to the domain. If you own http://www.myfrenchhats.com, your email addresses should be info@myfrenchhats.com or Jennifer@myfrenchhats.com or something similar because it's seen as more professional. If you have any employees who are using their Gmail or Yahoo! accounts to conduct business, get them a domain specific email and tell them to use it.

Get your business or location listed correctly on Google Local+ (previously known as Google Places and Google Maps)

I mentioned Google Street View and its objective of mapping the whole world in **Chapter 2: Ways That Social Media Will Affect You Whether You Use it or Not** so you realize you may already have a listing. Go to Google right now and look up the name of your business (you may need to type in the name of the business and the word "address" depending on how

Google is serving search results today). If you do, there will be a red pin on the map where you are. Go ahead, I'll wait for you.

Do you have one? If you do, you can claim it.

- Log into your Google account.
- Search for the name of your business (plus address, if necessary).
- Click on the red pin on the map. You should see a hovercard that pops up offering some info on your business.
- Look for the phrase "More Info." Somewhere on your listing, usually bottom right, is a question such as "Is this Your Business?" The wording may change but you can claim or manage this page from this button.

I'm going to stop this set of instructions here. Why? Google is notorious for changing things around, sometimes on a daily basis. While this book was being written in the summer and fall of 2012, Google was going through a changeover in branding and naming of this service.

If you look for driving directions online, you will see what they called Google Maps. If you are a business owner and submit your information, they called it Google Places. Drivers use Maps. Business owners use Places. When Google deployed their social network Google+ in 2011, they decided to switch many of their services to fit in with G+ and the renaming began. Places is now known as Google+ Local. Confused? You should be.

The link to get to Google Places is/was http://www.google.com/places. I've stopped giving you instructions because it was in flux as I wrote this. The best thing you can do if you get stuck is search for the term "help with Google Places" or "help with Google Local+." That will get you to the right place. (Sorry, unintended pun.)

It's important that you understand just how imperative it is to have this information listed correctly. Decision engines that help people navigate the world (Yelp, Ask.com and more) link up to Google Maps/Places/+Local and can give your customers business information including location, driving directions, phone numbers, hours of operation, coupons, pictures, videos and more.

Once you've claimed your location and filled in the correct information, you will need to confirm you are the rightful owner. This is normally done with a traditional postcard. It's counterintuitive, I know. But they send the postcard to the physical location and you must log into Google and enter the PIN number on the card to complete the confirmation. Once you've done that, the location is yours.

As far as maintenance, you don't need to update this much at all. I do think it's a good idea to check your listing once in awhile to see how it looks to others (because Google loves to change things) and if there is anything you'd like to update or rotate.

Get yourself listed on other directories

Google isn't the only game in town so I've given you a list of quite a few others that you can use to get the word out about where you are. This is really useful if you've had more than one location, ever worked from your home, or had your information posted incorrectly.

You don't need to use all of these; focus on the ones towards the top. You can claim many of them and correct your information for free. You don't need any of the paid services they offer unless you want to part yourself from your hard-earned money. Go the free route.

- Yahoo! http://www.yahoo.com/
- Bing http://www.bing.com/
- Yelp http://www.yelp.com/
- Merchant Circle http://www.merchantcircle.com/
- Manta (this is a **really** common search result site) http://www.manta.com/
- Facebook (get a business page and list your address) http://www.facebook.com
- Citysearch (check the default location and click Register to get started) http://www.citysearch.com
- MapQuest http://www.mapquest.com
- Foursquare https://foursquare.com/
- Yellowbook http://www.yellowbook.com/

- Yellowbot http://www.yellowbot.com/
- SuperPages http://www.superpages.com
- InsiderPages (sign up then search for your business, claim it, or create your listing) http://www.insiderpages.com/
- Local http://www.local.com/
- Localeze (search for your business, claim it or add a listing) http://webapp.localeze.com
- Angie's List http://www.angieslist.com
- Kudzu http://www.kudzu.com/
- Get Listed (an aggregate that will show you what your listings look like) http://getlisted.org/

Want a master list of directories? Try this: http://bit.ly/MasterListDirectories

Eliminate directory listings

You may have discovered in your vanity search, several directory listings that are incorrect or ones that you would like to eliminate. Some come from aggregate websites that list personal information already available on the web. One in particular has been brought up to me again and again, Spokeo.

I want to provide you with instructions on how to get rid of your listing there and once you've done it, you can understand the process on a variety of other sites where you are listed.

- Navigate to www.spokeo.com and enter your name. You may find that you have several listings. This information comes from public records such as utility bills, phone listings, and more. Investigate each listing that may possibly be you. You will see information such as gender, age, phone number, street address, and a photo of your neighborhood. In order to see the full results, they will charge you.

Don't pay! You can simply remove your listing. (You can read more about privacy rights on the web at Privacy Rights Clearinghouse[39] or about the $80,000 fine levied against Spokeo by the FTC.[40])

- Copy the listing URL out of the address bar and then navigate to www.spokeo.com/privacy
- Scroll down until you see "Removing Your Listing from Spokeo"
- Paste the URL into the Profile URL box and in the next box put an email address where you'll be receiving a confirmation link
- Enter in the Captcha phrase and Remove This Listing
- You should receive an email almost instantly that has a link saying "To complete the removal process, please click here." It works instantly.
- Now keep looking yourself up and repeating this process until they are all eliminated. I did it for myself and got rid of three listings in less than 5 minutes. Now do it for your spouse and kids.

When I repeated this process to make sure I got all my steps right for these instructions, I used my husband's information but had the link sent to my personal email address. Spokeo only allowed me to do 2 before it throttled me by saying "In order to prevent abuse, we must limit the frequency of automated privacy requests." **Don't let them stop you!** Go back in an hour or tomorrow and use an email that's associated to the person whose listing you are removing but eliminate all information that you can! Yes you can pay an outside service to do this for you but it will be much more expensive and time consuming than you'd like to believe.[41]

Other services with a similar information and process:

- ZoomInfo, to opt out use www.ZoomInfo.com/privacy
- 411.info, to opt out use www.411.info/privacy
- White Pages, to opt out use http://www.whitepagescustomers.com/get-help-with-a-personal-listing/

Other aggregator sites like Spokeo:
- Pipl or http://www.pipl.com
- Intelius or http://www.intelius.com

*Excerpt from "How to Remove Your Name from Online Listing Services" published on my blog and available here: http://kerryregoconsulting.com/2012/11/28/how-to-remove-your-name-from-online-listing-services/

Address negative content

Now that you have your directory listings up and running, you will want to go back to deal with negativity you've found online. If you haven't already, read **Chapter 3: How to Deal With Negative Online Feedback** to go about this in a way that will produce positive results.

I hear lots of concern about customer review sites like Yelp and the bad reviews that appear there. While it's a valid concern, the bad stuff is often a lot closer to home. Take a look at your comments on your blog or website or Facebook page. Often people are talking negatively about you because you simply aren't listening. Also, a lot of internet users are becoming better at spotting complainers or chronic whiners and those just looking to hurt people. If you have true problems to address in your business, they will appear online in the form of complaints. As a business owner, I wouldn't want to see that but I would take the opportunity to make some changes.

Create a strategy for using Social Media

This action plan chapter is designed for simple maintenance of your online reputation but I didn't want to leave you without a strategy for proactive Social Media use should you want one. You can get really fancy with this but I want to keep it easy for you. Here's my simple strategy, folks:

- **Goal**. What are you doing? What is the end result? What outcome do you desire? Iterate this information, communicate it to everyone you work with (if you're on a team), and keep it in front of you because it's easy to forget.

- **Know your audience**. Ask yourself the "5 W's"

   1. **WHO** is your target audience?
   2. **WHAT** do they want from you? **WHAT** value can you provide? **WHAT** do you want to write about?
   3. **WHEN** do they want to be reached? (time of day or week as well as time zone)
   4. **WHERE** are they? In other words, what tools are they using?
   5. **WHY** are you there? This is a reiteration of your goal or mission.

Don't know where your audience is spending their time? Take a look at **Chapter 5: Resources** (the blog resources specifically) as all of them provide great information in this arena. If I were to give you only one resource to help you know your audience and their habits better, it's Pew Research Center's Internet & American Life Project and can be found at http://www.pewinternet.org. They have studies and demographic data that will inspire and surprise you. I **love** this site.

- **Choose your tools.** Go back and reread **Chapter 2: What is Social Media?** for a full breakdown of the tools available to you. When you know your audience and research where they spend their time online, choosing your tools will be easier. This approach requires research, testing, and observation. Just because your audience historically uses a particular tool doesn't mean it's going to be the best choice for your needs. Sometimes you have to test them and observe out to know for sure.

- **Set a routine/Assign responsibility.** Who is going to write, post, and monitor? When will it be done? Simple. If you don't set this (and put the tasks on your calendar), it won't happen. This is when you use your editorial calendar.

- **Measure.** In order to know if you've achieved your goals (step one of strategy), you will need to measure your performance. I recommend that you do this when performing your monthly processes such as reconciliation or inventory. This enables easy month-over-month comparisons for reporting. By all means, you can look at your numbers more frequently than once per month but it can hinder creativity and free-thinking if you are always worried about how your actions will affect your analytics.

  If you don't already have one, build a process sheet and put Social Media metrics on there. I have included a sample metric report in this **Chapter 5: Resources**. Not all measurements are created equally. Your metrics should match your goals and this is unique for each person or organization. If you work for someone else, these measurements will allow you to create a report that helps the decision makers see patterns about what is and is not working. You **must** track performance to know if what you are doing is worth your time.

- **Adjust.** Why would you possibly need to do this? No one gets it right the first time. Things on the internet never stop changing and you will learn a tremendous amount by measuring your results and making adjustments as necessary.

- **PERSIST**. I believe all of these steps are important but this final step is a deal breaker. I compare it to going to the gym. If you workout every day for a week, you wouldn't expect a six-pack, would you? Many believe that they should see fantastic results online within minutes or days and that's simply not realistic. Give it six months of true effort and you'll see positive results. Truthfully, you should see results much faster than that depending on what tools you are using but giving yourself that long view helps to manage your expectations. Don't give up!

Post original content to Social Media channels

You only get one reputation, so be proactive! Once content exists on the web about you, it's very difficult to get it removed. Rather than fight the tide, I say the best plan of action is to put up your own content. Why? Search engines take into account the age of the material, the popularity of the originating site, and whether the content is coming from the source (you writing about you), among other things. If someone says something bad about you, posting your own original words will give you a good chance of pushing that person's search result down the page further and further away from page one, which is as far as most people go. Consistent posting about you, your brand, or other original work ensures that your words come up before that of others.

Google, as the number one search engine, highly values content coming from Social Media platforms. It gets "Google Juice" from the tools that publish quickly and are designed for up-to-date information. Google's first objective is to provide fresh and accurate search results (it may or may not achieve this). It values subject matter that aligns with this goal.

Editorial Calendar

But what do you write about? In **Chapter 5: Resources**, I provide a basic editorial calendar that you will be able to create yourself in Excel that gives you a 12-month plan. Pick a subject for each month and plug in the channels you are using. It allows you to map out the focus of your communication, the distribution, and timing. You can make it more detailed by including who will be writing and any other information you prefer. There's a blog I wrote "15 Easy Blog Post Topics" that will provide you with a go-to list of content that never gets old which can be used on any Social Media channel http://bit.ly/KRCeasyblog. Read the blog to get a more in-depth explanation of how to address these subjects but here's the list:

- Seasons, weather, and holidays
- Your industry's busy or quiet time
- Industry related events
- Education
- Employee features
- Vendors and partners
- Case study and/or client success story
- Testimonials and interviews
- Product release
- Hot topics
- History or story of your company
- Differentiate yourself from your competition
- Identify obstacles and solutions
- Survey
- Frequently asked questions

An easier version is to simply print out the calendar you use for work and circle the items you'd like to promote or talk about that are coming up (or have occurred in the past). I use color-coding to keep track of where I've promoted the information. You can actually see how I do that here: http://bit.ly/KRCeasycalendar

Setup an internal Social Media communications policy

We talked about this in **Chapter 3: Why You Must Have a Communications Policy**. This policy won't apply just to social networking or internet sites. This will cover phone, email, fax, letter, face-to-face, Social Media and other forms of communication your industry requires. Make sure you have an up-to-date, clear policy about what is or is not acceptable.

Review this with your team. Please don't assume they know what's expected of them.

Create a Crisis plan

Not only does this relate to Social Media and your online assets, crisis plans should apply to your entire business (**see next section: Legacy and Process Management**). Think of it like an emergency services department would: go through the full exercise of the worst case scenario(s) and what you will do if/when your website or Social Media channels get hacked[42]. You and your team will have muscle memory and by drilling it several times, you will increase the ease with which you and your team are able to adapt to an online crisis situation.

Also **see Chapter 2: The Viral Nature of a Social Media Crisis**

Review your online assets

Don't take for granted that it's working. Go through your website and other assets with a fine toothed comb. Click on every link and review all information. Check it out from multiple devices and browsers. Your website may look or perform differently in Internet Explorer than Firefox and will definitely look different on a mobile device than it will on a desktop computer You **will** find something that doesn't work, is broken, needs an update, is out of date, or is incorrect. I like to review pages on my website out of order so that you don't miss things that normally would be in sequence. Like the "auto-fill" function, your brain will make assumptions and miss things. Another reason this is a good idea is because visitors come to your website from all angles. They enter and navigate through your site in a different order than you expect.

It's a great idea to put this task on your process list on a regular basis. You choose if you want to review monthly or quarterly but since Google searches and reads your site six to eight times per month, it behooves you to make this a frequent task. When you make changes to your site, Google rewards you with higher search results for fresh information.

Assess your customers with a survey

It may seem simple but ask your clients and customers how they prefer that you communicate with them. The information you will gain from this one question is extremely valuable. It doesn't have to be a postcard or a digital survey. It can be worked into everyday conversations, sales calls, or your current follow-up process.

I stumbled across this one by accident. I was in a session with a client and recalled feeling frustrated with not knowing how to reliably reach her. I figured I'd ask her what worked best. She said she loved email and never answered her phone. It dawned on me then that we'd worked together for years but I'd never spoken to her on the phone. **It's not always what you want: it's what your customers prefer.**

Asking new customers how they found your service is great for tracking of conversions. The answers are often ones you've never knew about. Sometimes another company or service has placed you on its site or mentioned you and now you can now thank them for the referral. This may also aid you in uncovering your Super Fans. These are the people that sing your praises but never tell you they are referring you to everyone they know. If you learn of one of these people, make sure you thank them and take good care of them because they are an unpaid salesperson. Keep them in the loop on new products, projects, and information.

Get content deleted from the web

If you are bound and determined to get your name or content relating to you deleted from the web, I found an article that will walk you through it. Because I've never used this particular process myself, I will simply provide you with the link and let you give it a shot:
http://howto.cnet.com/8301-11310_39-57417419-285/how-to-delete-yourself-from-the-internet/

My belief is that once it's up, it's up. But a determined soul may achieve deletion. Good luck!

~

LEGACY AND PROCESS MANAGEMENT

In my previous life, I was an organization expert with an emphasis on technology. When the iPhone came out, it changed what my clients wanted from me. This is an excerpt from a blog I wrote that I think compliments the content of this book, and speaks to the way I think about business. I want to share it with you. Take what you need and leave what doesn't apply. Consider it a bonus.

Have you ever been sick unexpectedly? Had an accident that prevented you from work? Was your business able to cope with your absence? I started to think long and hard about the process of my work years ago when I was in member relations and accounting at a country club while I prepared to go on maternity leave. I had taken on many tasks and knew quirks of my job and business inside and out. My goal was to leave my team as informed as possible so they needed to call me for nothing. I achieved this by documenting my tasks well and I'll tell you how you can do the same. When you lose someone for a day, a week, or forever, you will be able to function just fine.[43]

Legacy management

Have everyone in your office track their day from beginning to end. Tape a piece of paper to your desk if you sit at one; that way it won't fly off as you move things around. Every day for a week, track your tasks in chronological order. When you've written down all the tasks, describe how to do them in detail. Write it like someone is going to use your notes, like a recipe, to do your job. Include the instructions on how you turn the alarm system on and off, how to perform a backup of the computer system, how to do a bank drop, details, codes, passwords, whatever your duties entail. When everyone has completed this, create a manual that is centrally located and alert the appropriate people as to the book's whereabouts. Due to the manual's sensitive nature, everyone needn't be privy to its location, but make sure several people know so that if one is out sick and the other gets hit by a bus, you're covered.

Business information

In that central manual you've created, it's a good idea to include the mission statement, contact information for boards or owners, your insurance policy with agent name, alarms, utility companies, staff list with contact info, and other emergency information. Provide a map of your location(s). List regular vendors and visitors (this also can be helpful in narrowing down theft).

Review your assets

You may very well have this information recorded somewhere as a part of your insurance paperwork. Use that list or start one that inventories all your assets such as furniture, all technology, vehicles, paperwork, and anything else that would need to be replaced in the event of a theft, fire, flood, hurricane, power surge or other physical disaster.

Assess your computer systems security

Hire an expert to spot the problem areas and security concerns that leave you exposed. This may be necessary for you to perform if you accept contact information, payment information, or other sensitive data that require you to be legally compliant.

Cloud computing

If you have a mobile or dispersed team, investigate the usefulness of cloud storage. Tools like Dropbox, Basecamp, Evernote, Google Drive and others give you the ability to work, share documents, and collaborate anywhere on the planet. With backup servers, these systems can sometimes be safer than your own.

Have you updated your software, hardware, antivirus protection, or done a maintenance check recently? Not only does cloud computing provide offsite security (helpful in case of a natural disaster like a fire or flood that affects your location), enhanced computing power, increased storage capacity, easier collaboration with distant teammates, they provide upgrades and maintenance of the larger system so you don't need a large tech department. And the cost of these tools can be very affordable. Many start free or are very low cost, can be on a month-to-month payment, and if you want enhanced features you pay more.

Cloud security

This is a growing area of concern. CloudLock, Cyber Ark, and Cipher Cloud are all tools that provide secure ways to partake of cloud services. LastPass will help you contain all of your keywords within one system.

Just so you know, no system is perfect. Everyone gets hacked sooner or later (knock on wood). It's just the way life is. Remember, there is no such thing as complete control. Even NASA got hacked 13 times in 2011.[44] You can take appropriate steps to mitigate your risk. I've used many computers (belonging to others) that were unprotected, out-of-date, contained the remnants of their owner's risky internet activities, and were generally unsafe. Just because you have your own server or LAN (local area network) doesn't make your system safer than one on which you lease space.

Software-as-a-service

This is a subcategory of cloud computing. Examples of tools that could increase the efficiency of your operation include Google Voice or Skype for voice communications (both start at free and go up), Myfax for online fax (it cuts down on paper, ink, and the amount of equipment needed), Quickbooks online, Salesforce, and so many more. These services can drastically reduce your monthly budget and eliminate the large number of computer software licenses needed for your operation.

Mobile security

Considering the tremendous amount of sensitive information being accessed via mobile devices, it's prudent to ask: How secure are they? McAfee issued a report in 2012 that Android devices are the most at risk and suffer the most breaches.[45] Part of the reason for constant updates and upgrades is to stay ahead of the bad guys.

Website and Social Media inventory

With the high use of internet tools in the workplace today, most managers don't think to require login information from employees and staff. If you don't have their passwords when they are out, think of the problems that could quickly spiral out of control. This is of the utmost importance in brand communications when using Social Media tools.

Multiple admins on accounts such as Facebook pages and shared login information will help prevent damage when one "goes postal." It used to be when someone was fired, she might sabotage a filing system or steal supplies. Now that person can post the worst thing you can think of on a high profile site like Twitter, Facebook, or YouTube. When someone is let go, have her hand over her keys, remove her admin status, and **change passwords to accounts she had access to before she leaves the building**. Make these changes preferably before you have "the conversation" because she can pick up her mobile device and do damage as she's walking back to her desk to clean it out. These are vital steps, especially if you suspect the person will go off the rails or is ending on anything less than a happy note.

Social Media sensitivity training

Due to the relatively new web-based tools we are working with, the majority of your staff may have had little exposure and could be falling behind. You may need to invest in training to remain competitive. Don't be afraid to invest in that training. Your business will benefit.

*Excerpt from "Legacy and Process Management: Steps to Take" and is available at: http://kerryregoconsulting.com/2012/03/12/legacy-and-process-management-steps-to-take/

~

CONCLUSION

The content included in this book is a combination of what I talk about in my classes, blogs I've written, important information I believe you should know, and steps to help you take control.

I am passionate about this subject and want to provide you with the tools to help you become empowered. Many people are worried and frightened by what they don't know, especially when it comes to technology. I know when you have education and a plan, you can overcome what scares you.

I am here for you. Good luck!

CHAPTER 5:

RESOURCES

RESOURCES

Books

- Anderson, Chris Anderson, *Free: The Future of a Radical Price. Free: The Future of a Radical Price.* Hyperion, 2009

- Brogan,Chris, Smith,Julien *Trust Agents: Using the Web to Build Influence, Improve Reputation, and Earn Trust.* Wiley, 2010

- Joel, Mitch *Six Pixels of Separation: Everyone is Connected. Connect Your Business to Everyone.* Business Plus, 2010

- Gladwell, Malcolm, *The Outliers,* Back Bay Books, 2011

- Heath, Chip and Heath, Dan, *Made to Stick: Why Some Ideas Survive and Others Die.* New York: Random House, 2007

Blogs

- *Mashable* | Social Media News and Web Tips
  http://mashable.com/

- *TechCrunch*
  http://techcrunch.com/

- *Slashdot* | News for nerds, stuff that matters.
  http://slashdot.org/

- *Facebook Help Center* | Facebook
  https://www.facebook.com/help/

- *GCFLearning* | Your Free Learning Resource.
  http://www.gcflearnfree.org/

Other Resources

- *YouTube*
  http://www.youtube.com

- *Pew Internet* | Pew Research Center's Internet & American Life Project
  http://pewinternet.org/

- *Web4Biz* | Social Media Management Workshop
  http://web4biz.org

- *Web4Biz YouTube Channel* | Free Videos of Tech Training with Kerry Rego
  http://www.youtube.com/Web4BizOrg

- Editorial calendar (next page) to be used with blog "15 Easy Blog Topics" found at http://kerryregoconsulting.com/2012/01/23/15-easy-blog-post-topics/

- Metric report (two pages away)

EDITORIAL CALENDAR

Marketing Editorial Calendar

	Theme	Blog	Email Mrkt	Facebook	Instagram
January '13	History/Story of Company				
February '13	Primary Service				
March '13	Educational Conference				
April '13	Community Service				
May '13	Secondary Service				
June '13	Client Success Story/Testimonial				
July '13	Differentiate				
August '13	Primary Service				
September '13	Communication				
October '13	Employees				
November '13	Secondary Service				
December '13	Holiday				
More ideas?	http://bit.ly/KRCeasyblog				

Google Analytics	January	February	March	April
Visits				
Unique Visits				
bounce rate				
avg time on site				
pages per visit				
#1 source of traffic				
Facebook				
Fans				
Unsubscribes				
sources of traffic				
Viral Post				
Google Analytics/Visits				
Twitter				
Followers				
RT's/Favs				
Blog				
Subscribers				
Comments				
YouTube				
Subscribers				
Channel Views				
Upload Views				
Performance				
Favorited				
Comments				
Traffic Source				

Google Local/Places	January	February	March	April
Impressions				
Actions				
Top search queries				
Constant Contact				
Email List				
Added self to list				
Opens				
Bounces				
Spam				
Opt Out				
Forward				
Clicks				
#1 clickthrough				
SM shares				
Yelp				
Page Views				
LinkedIn				
Company Followers				
Pinterest				
Followers				
Pinfluence				
Klout				

BIBLIOGRAPHY

1. Eric Schmidt, "Every 2 Days We Create As Much Information As We Did up To 2003," *Crunchbase* (blog), August 4, 2010, http://techcrunch.com/2010/08/04/schmidt-data/.
2. "Reputation Management", *Wikipedia*, last modified November 5, 2012, http://en.wikipedia.org/wiki/Reputation_management.
3. "One in Five Technology Firms Has Rejected a Job Applicant Because Of Social Media Profile-Eurocom Worldwide Annual Survey," *Eurocom Worldwide* (blog), March 3, 2012, http://www.eurocompr.com/prfitem.asp?id=14921.
4. Julianne Pepitone, " Android races past Apple in smartphone market share," *CNN Money* (blog), August 9, 2012 (10:03 a.m.), http://money.cnn.com/2012/08/08/technology/smartphone-market-share/.
5. Philip Gordon and Lauren Woon, "Re-Thinking and Rejecting Social Media "Password Protection" Legislation," *Workplace Privacy Counsel*, (blog) *Privacy and Data Protection Practice Group,* July 10, 2012, http://privacyblog.littler.com/tags/stored-communications-act/.
6. Adrianne Jeffries, " As Banks Start Nosing Around Facebook and Twitter, The Wrong Friends Might Just Sink Your Credit," *BetaBeat,* (blog), December 13, 2011 (7:39 p.m.), http://betabeat.com/2011/12/as-banks-start-nosing-around-facebook-and-twitter-the-wrong-friends-might-just-sink-your-credit/.
7. Steve McLellan, Company Reputation Translates Into Stock Value," *Media Daily News*, (blog), March 16, 2012 (11:03 a.m.), http://www.mediapost.com/publications/article/170349/company-reputation-translates-into-stock-value.html.
8. "United Breaks Guitars," *Wikipedia*, last modified October 31, 2012, http://en.wikipedia.org/wiki/United_Breaks_Guitars.
9. "CAN-SPAM Act of 2003," *Wikipedia*, last modified September 19, 2012, http://en.wikipedia.org/wiki/CAN-SPAM_Act_of_2003.
10. Kerry Rego, "Gamification: The Greatest Call to Action" *Kerry Rego Consulting*, (blog), November 7, 2012

http://kerryregoconsulting.com/2012/11/07/gamification-the-greatest-call-to-action/

11. Hollis Thomases, "Customer Service Now Matters More," *Inc.*, (blog), May 25, 2012, http://www.inc.com/hollis-thomases/customer-service-now-matters-more.html.

12. Audio Archive, "Audio Archive: Security and Transparency, Business and Social Media," *Sustainable Business Forum*, (blog), August 19, 2011, http://sustainablebusinessforum.com/audio-archive-security-transparency-business-social-media.

13. Joanna Brenner, "Social Networking (full detail)," *Pew Internet*, (blog), September 17, 2012, http://pewinternet.org/Commentary/2012/March/Pew-Internet-Social-Networking-full-detail.aspx.

14. Jennifer Beese, "Why Brick and Mortar Retailers Need To Adopt Digital Marketing," SproutSocial, (blog), August 10, 2012, http://sproutsocial.com/insights/2012/08/retail-digital-marketing/.

15. "Social Media Raises the Stakes for Customer Service," American Express, (blog), May 2, 2012, http://about.americanexpress.com/news/pr/2012/gcsb.aspx.

16. Allegra Tepper, " The Power of Text Message Marketing," Mashable Business, (blog), July 13, 2012, http://mashable.com/2012/07/13/text-message-marketing-infographic/.

17. Liz Powell, "Death Becomes The Phone Book," White Pages, (blog), http://blog.whitepages.com/2011/12/28/death-becomes-the-phone-book/.

18. Tom Evslin, "TAC to FCC: Set a Date Certain for the End of the PSTN," *Fractals of Change*, (blog), http://blog.tomevslin.com/2011/07/tac-to-fcc-set-a-date-certain-for-the-end-of-the-pstn.html.

19. David Cay Johnston, "RPT-COLUMN-An end to phones in every home?,"(blog), *Reuters*, March 28, 2012, http://www.reuters.com/article/2012/03/28/column-dcjohnston-phone-idUSL2E8EROHD20120328.

20. Stephen J. Blumberg, Ph.D., and Julian V. Luke, "Wireless Substitution: Early Release of Estimates From the National Health

Interview Survey, January–June 2011," *CDC*, released December 21, 2011, http://www.cdc.gov/nchs/data/nhis/earlyrelease/wireless201112.pdf.

21. 'Google Street View*" Wikipedia*, last modified November 9, 2012, http://en.wikipedia.org/wiki/Google_Street_View.

22. Kerry Rego, "Are You Cool Enough to Get Service? Klout Score Leads to Classism," *Kerry Rego Consulting*, (blog), October 2, 2010, http://kerryregoconsulting.com/2010/10/02/are-you-cool-enough-to-get-service-klout-score-leads-to-classism/.

23. Kerry Rego, "Don't Drink and Post!" *Kerry Rego Consulting*, (blog), June 29, 2011, http://kerryregoconsulting.com/2011/06/29/dont-drink-and-post/

24. Tim Nudd, "ChapStick Gets Itself in a Social Media Death Spiral A brand's silent war against its Facebook fans," *ADFREAK*, (blog), October 26, 2011, http://www.adweek.com/adfreak/chapstick-gets-itself-social-media-death-spiral-136097.

25. "Technophobia," *Wikipedia*, last modified November 6, 2012, http://en.wikipedia.org/wiki/Technophobia.

26. Kathryn Zickuhr, " Generations," *Pew Internet*, (blog), December 16, 2010, http://www.pewinternet.org/Reports/2010/Generations-2010.aspx.

27. Kathryn Zickuhr, Mary Madden, "Older adults and internet use," *Pew Internet*, (blog), June 6, 2012, http://pewinternet.org/Reports/2012/Older-adults-and-internet-use.aspx.

28. Eric Durban, "Agriculture finding its voice on social media," *Harvest*, (blog), November 4, 2011, http://harvestpublicmedia.org/blog/859/agriculture-finding-its-voice-social-media/5.

29. Joann Pan, "Social Media-Connected Teens Seek Time Offline [STUDY]," *Mashable*, (blog), June 26, 2012, http://mashable.com/2012/06/26/social-media-teens/.

30. Jennifer Cowher Williams, "Annual Sleep in America Poll Exploring Connections with Communications Technology Use and Sleep," *National Sleep Foundation*, (blog), March 7, 2011,

http://www.sleepfoundation.org/article/press-release/annual-sleep-america-poll-exploring-connections-communications-technology-use-

31. Kerry Rego, " The Antidote To Technology," *Kerry Rego Consulting*, (blog), April 29, 2012, http://kerryregoconsulting.com/2012/04/29/the-antidote-to-technology/.

32. Abraham Maslow, *Wikipedia*, last revised November 6, 2012, http://en.wikipedia.org/wiki/Abraham_Maslow.

33. "2011 Survey Results", *IACP Center For Social Media*, September 2011, http://www.iacpsocialmedia.org/Resources/Publications/2011SurveyResults.aspx.

34. Jack Dorsey, "Talked with NYPD Commissioner Ray Kelly about Twitter & Square. And the Twitter board in the command center," *Twyla*, (blog), May 28, 2011, http://www.twylah.com/jack/tweets/52515134727401472.

35. "Astroturfing*," Wikipedia*, last modified November 7, 2012, http://en.wikipedia.org/wiki/Astroturfing.

36. Kerry Rego, "Be Transparent: Why Deleting Negative Posts is a Bad Idea", *Kerry Rego Consulting*, (blog), June 22, 2012, http://kerryregoconsulting.com/2012/06/22/be-transparent-why-deleting-negative-posts-is-a-bad-idea/.

37. Kerry Rego, "The Lady Test: Privacy, Decorum and Online Behavior", *Kerry Rego Consulting*, (blog), August 13, 2010, http://kerryregoconsulting.com/2010/08/13/the-lady-test-privacy-decorum-and-online-behavior/.

38. Jin Han, "February 2012 US Search Market Share Report," *Compete Pulse*, (blog), March 8, 2012, http://blog.compete.com/2012/03/08/february-2012-us-search-market-share-report/.

39. "Online Information Brokers and Your Privacy", *Privacy Rights Clearinghouse,* revised February 2011, https://www.privacyrights.org/ar/infobrokers.htm

40. "Spokeo to Pay $800,000 to Settle FTC Charges Company Allegedly Marketed Information to Employers and Recruiters in Violation of

FCRA", *Federal Trade Commission*, June 12, 2012,
http://ftc.gov/opa/2012/06/spokeo.shtm

41. Kerry Rego, "How to Remove Your Name from Online Listing
    Services", *Kerry Rego Consulting*, (blog), November 28, 2012,
    http://kerryregoconsulting.com/2012/11/28/how-to-remove-your-
    name-from-online-listing-services/

42. Dallas Lawrence, "What to Do When Your Website Gets Hacked,"
    Mashable Business, (blog) February 2, 2012,
    http://mashable.com/2012/02/02/website-hacked-help/.

43. Kerry Rego, "Legacy and Process Management: Steps to Take",
    Kerry Rego Consulting, (blog), March 12, 2012,
    http://kerryregoconsulting.com/2012/03/12/legacy-and-process-
    management-steps-to-take/.

44. "NASA Hacked 13 Times Last Year, Space Agency Says*," Reuters*,
    (blog), last modified March 2, 2012 (3:03 p.m.), —
    http://www.huffingtonpost.com/2012/03/02/nasa-hack-
    2011_n_1316797.html.

45. Taylor Armerding, "Threat reports finger Android again*," CSO Data
    Protection*, (blog), September 6, 2012,
    http://www.csoonline.com/article/715489/threat-reports-finger-
    android-again.

KERRY REGO CONSULTING SERVICES

You may choose to take on these tasks yourself. You absolutely can do everything listed in this book but I understand if you are overwhelmed. If you would like to know how I might be of service to you, read on.

I provide a range of services in four categories:

1. **Education**
   Individual and group lessons
   Classes, custom, and preset
   Keynote presentations for events

2. **Implementation**
   Building brand presences on Facebook pages, Twitter, YouTube, LinkedIn, and Pinterest; creation of customized Reputation Management tools, and more

3. **Training**
   Hands-on instruction of how to navigate and maintain accounts

4. **Support**
   Continued education and assistance with implementation as tools continue to change

TESTIMONIALS

"She has an amazing knack of presenting the basics, including the history of social media and how it's being used in many ways."
Diane Judd, Professional Organizer

"When you work with Kerry, you know you are getting the best. She is Sonoma County's expert on social media. Her thirst for leading the knowledge curve is apparent in every interaction."
Elaina Hunt, Director of Marketing, Summit State Bank

"Kerry Rego is one of the est speakers I have ever hear. She is passionate, engages her audience and knows her material."
Bill Allen, VP Marketing and Sales, Managed Signals

"Her (Excel) instruction was straightforward and easy to understand. Kerry is extremely knowledgeable. And I am very grateful for her methodical and comfortable style."
Ann Bouligny, Channel HR

"Thank you for your excellent service over the past two years to our non-profit. Your expertise and creative energy were invaluable in making our work effective and really getting our message out."
Sharon Anderson, Former Director, Bay Area Funeral Society

"I was captivated by your presentation on social networking. Thanks for your energetic and informative presentation. It was refreshing."
Kimberly Hanley, Wellness Consultant

"For people starting at square one using technology: Kerry has a great way of making everything 'logical'...meeting clients where they are at...and shows patience in getting them where they want to go."
Dian Nunes, T&D Associates

I WANT TO HEAR FROM YOU!

As the reader of this book, you are my most important critic. I value your opinion and want to know what I'm doing right, what I could do better, what subject matter you'd like to see me write about, and anything else you think I should know about.

Please note that I am available as a consultant to guide you through the process of applying the tools discussed in this book. Please contact my team to set up an arrangement for my services.

When you write, please be sure to include at least a portion of this book's title as well as your name, email address, and any other communication channel of your choice. I will carefully review your comments personally.

Email: book@kerryregoconsulting.com

Mail:
Kerry Rego Consulting
394 Tesconi Court, Suite 107
Santa Rosa, CA 95401 USA

Social Media:
http://www.facebook.com/KerryRegoConsulting
http://twitter.com/kregobiz
http://gplus.to/KerryRego
http://www.pinterest.com/kregobiz

Made in the USA
Charleston, SC
09 December 2012